Dear Friend:

Thank you for writing to us during our annual
LETTER WEEK. It's always a special joy and
encouragement to hear from our friends.

It's my pleasure to send this special edition of
CHRISTIAN PERSPECTIVES ON
CONTROVERSIAL ISSUES written by our own
radio pastor, Donald Cole,

In these days of compromise, it's important for the
Christian to know the biblical view we should be
taking in facing today's controversial issues.

I believe Pastor Cole faces these issues head-on.
His thoughtful insights are the result of his keen
social awareness, careful research, and a
thorough knowledge of God's Word.

Thank you again for your faithful expressions of
interest and support in the ministries of Moody
Bible Institute.

Your Friend,

George Sweeting

Christian Perspectives on Controversial Issues

by
C. Donald Cole

MOODY PRESS
CHICAGO

1 2 3 4 5 6 7 Printing/LC/Year 87 86 85 84 83 82

Printed in the United States of America

Contents

1

The American Family

More than fifty thousand women in summery white outfits gathered in Chicago's Grant Park to show their support for the Equal Rights Amendment. According to reports, the mood was upbeat; the women were optimistic about ERA's chances in the Illinois House of Representatives. They were also determined, and they wanted the world to know that they were not *begging;* they were *demanding* equal rights. Politicians who oppose ERA were warned that they would find themselves turfed out of office by women voters.

Later that day, I passed a vanload of women leaving Chicago. Since ERA was chalked on the windows, I assumed that they were going home after the rally, or were headed for Springfield to lobby for passage of the bill. Before long, I pulled off the road to let Naomi drive for a while. The next time we passed the van, its passengers on the left saw me slouched in the passenger seat, with my wife at the steering wheel. The incident got me thinking about some of the issues raised by the continuing agitation over the passage of ERA.

I am not (n-o-t, not) going to talk about ERA. Not this time. Our subject is the American family, and the only point in mentioning ERA is that these separate issues are frequently mentioned in the same breath, usually by opponents of ERA, who contend that passage of the bill

7

would further undermine the already weakened American family. I do not pause to discuss the validity of the charge; my subject is the American family itself.

I am interested, however, in the concept of "family-policy," which, says Allan C. Carlson, "has generated numerous proposals aimed at strengthening family life through government actions."[1] Family-policy advocates point to evidence that the family is in trouble—the increasing number of divorces, working mothers, teenage pregnancies, single-parent homes, and unmarried couples that live together. No doubt you have seen articles on each of these topics. If not, start looking for them in the newspaper. Before long, you'll have a little pile of clippings recording various aspects of the breakup of the American family and perhaps offering proposals for government action, calculated to reverse the process or compensate for it.

Why is the family in such deep trouble? Men and women who think about the problem suggest at least three plausible answers: first, widespread contempt for, or indifference to, traditions. Says David A. Goslin, who directed a study of the family for the National Academy of Sciences, "Now people have more options—to get married or not, to have children or not, to stay married or not, to work or not."[2] The options exist largely because of indifference to traditions, and also because of economic conditions. In the past, it would not have occurred to many couples to try to solve their marital problems in a divorce court; they thrashed them out in customary ways,

[1]Allan C. Carlson, "Families, Sex, and the Liberal Agenda," *The Public Interest*, no. 58, Winter 1980, p. 62.

[2]David A. Goslin, quoted by Kenneth L. Woodward, "Saving the Family," *Newsweek*, 15 May 1978, p. 64.

or they learned to adjust to them. However, if they did seek relief in the courts, they were generally rebuffed. Now all is changed; for the poor, at least, it's easier to get a divorce than a mortgage. The courts have adjusted to changing attitudes, reflecting widespread indifference to biblical teaching about the sanctity of marriage.

A second cause of trouble in the family is financial. Young people see statistical charts indicating the total cost of raising a child from birth through college. Statisticians tell prospective parents that it will cost tens of thousands of dollars to rear a child. Inevitably, many couples either postpone having children until they have money in the bank, which takes a long time, or they limit the number of children to one or two.

Such anxiety about the bare cost of rearing children probably reflects changing values and a subtle selfishness that masquerades as concern for the welfare of a growing child. Many young couples are not really worried about the cost of a child for the child's sake. They aren't worried about being able to provide for children; they're concerned that the cost might reduce their personal standard of living. "This is an awful time to bring a child into the world," some say. The truth is, it's as good a time as any in history. Never was there a worse time than when Moses was born; boy babies were under the ban. Yet when he was born, Moses' parents kept him alive, hidden from all who would kill him. Why? Because he was a beautiful baby! Who needs a better reason? They were not afraid of the king's edict to kill all of the Hebrew male babies; they trusted in God (Hebrews 11:23). For the same reason, Christian couples, at least, should not be afraid to create God-honoring families—two-parent families in which children are welcomed as gifts from the Lord (cf. Psalm 127:3-5). It's as silly to worry about the total cost of rearing children as about the total cost of a mortgage. You pay it a little at a time.

A third source of trouble in the family is parental loss of control to competitors—television, school, and peer groups. It isn't easy to say which competitor exerts the greatest influence on a child. It's probably a toss-up between television and the school, though the school (that is, the public school) has been exerting its influence in opposition to parental influence considerably longer than television. Experts trained in the schools are also competitors. The existence of experts in virtually everything, with their influence, is really an extension of the role of the school in attempting to do what, in modern theory, the family cannot. Says Christopher Lasch, "By convincing the housewife, and finally her husband, to rely on outside technology and the advice of outside experts, the apparatus of mass tuition—the successor to the church in our secularized society—has undermined the family's capacity to provide for itself."[3]

Please don't misunderstand me. I am not decrying recourse to experts. I myself read Dr. Spock's *Baby Book* every time we had a new baby in the house. We lived in Africa, and his book was invaluable for formulas, suggestions for treating diaper rash or diarrhea, and reassurance when we didn't know what was ailing the child. Conceivably, that expert physician saved our children's lives more than once, and, without a question, he contributed to our own peace of mind. However, it did not occur to us that we were inadequate as parents, or that we needed help from Dr. Spock in understanding the children and in knowing the values we wanted to inculcate in them. We

[3]Christopher Lasch, *The Culture of Narcissism: American Life in an Age of Diminishing Expectations* (New York: Norton, 1978).

were still what we still are, Christians, and we intended to raise our children to be Christians, to the extent that this was possible.

Does this mean that we were completely self-sufficient and did not need advice? Of course not! However, most normally intelligent couples who were themselves nourished in the church, soaking up the moral values taught in the Bible, know almost instinctively how to rear their children. Everybody makes mistakes, to be sure, but a couple who learned values in the church will probably make fewer serious mistakes than their neighbors who don't go to church at all, including unchurched child psychologists.

Young couples living in our times are fortunate; they have access to a wealth of materials that were not available when my wife and I, and our peers, were bringing up children. Check any Christian bookstore for listings, and you'll see what I mean. I recall chuckling over something in one of Dr. James Dobson's books not long ago, thinking, "Ah, yes, how true! And how sad that I didn't know that twenty years ago! Reading it now is like locking the barn door after the horse is stolen."

You see that I am not belittling experts—just the wrong experts. If, as an Israelite parent in ancient times, you learn God's Word and teach it to your children, you will have placed them squarely in the right path (Deuteronomy 4:10; 6:7). Whether they stay there, following in your moral footsteps, is up to them. But getting them started is the responsibility of parents; for this, little or no advice from professionally trained experts is needed. If you run into trouble (and you may; certainly life is more complicated now than in ancient Israel's agrarian society), ask your friends in church for help. Sooner or later, someone will open up and admit that he also had the same problem with his child. He'll tell you what he learned, and he'll lend you a book that helped him, and he'll pray with you.

You don't need the government's help in rearing your children, although if the secular society around you has seduced your child or children into taking drugs or swigging beer to the point of alcoholism, you may want to avail yourself of federal or local programs designed to remedy the problem. Secular experts know a great deal about the drug culture, alcoholism, crime, and such ills. Those are their fields. However, we do not need the legislation now being proposed by family-policy advocates for strengthening the family; we do not believe their proposals (income redistribution, guaranteed minimum incomes, integrated social services, better sex education, and the like) will really help to build families.

Then what will legislation proposed by family-policy advocates do? Allan C. Carlson writes, "The disconcerting reality appears to be that state social intervention on behalf of families actually weakens or destroys families."[4] If this is true of social programs already on the books, what will happen if we get more of the same? The answer is obvious: further weakening of the family.

Is Carlson right? I think he is. In his view, American families are being weakened by two forces (in addition to the three listed earlier in this talk): from within, "by the impact of the . . . sex revolution on male-female ties and on the linkage of generations;" and from without, "by the cultural abandonment of the nuclear-family norm and the normative embrace of amoral family and sexual ethics by elements of the educated upper-middle class."[5] Nothing

[4]Carlson, p. 79.
[5]Ibid., p. 78.

the government can do can check or reverse these trends. Furthermore, the proposals that have been made (income redistribution, day-care centers, sex education) would tend to confirm society in its "embrace of amoral family and sexual ethics"; they would not strengthen families.

If the government can't strengthen families, who can? Dr. Ted Ward, professor of Curriculum Research at Michigan State University, describes what the church, "the pillar and support of the truth" (1 Timothy 3:15), can do to strengthen families. The church, he says, needs to be

> a prophetic voice in the pulpit reminding us of what God says about the nature of the family. . . . When this prophetic voice is boldly keyed to God's righteous nature of mercy, love, and justice, the Christian family will become a real contrast to the secular family—the viable option that is muffled and foggy today.[6]

In the secular world, the traditional family is viewed as "having been pragmatically useful in the past but expendable in the present."[7] This, in all likelihood, is the view government programs will seek to establish. If you agree with me that the secular view is wrong, you'll have little or no sympathy for proposals for legislation set forth by family-policy advocates. How should we register our disapproval? The best expression is a strong family, built and maintained according to norms set up in the Bible.

[6]Ted Ward, "The Christian Family at Late Century," *Evangelical Newsletter*, 24 October 1975, p. 4.

[7]Ibid.

2

Should Mothers Work?

In April 1979, Jane Byrne was elected mayor of Chicago. About a month later, another woman was given an even bigger assignment: Margaret Thatcher won the election in Britain and was asked by the Queen to form a new government, with herself as Prime Minister. Men everywhere wondered what the world was coming to, and in some churches, two questions were discussed with due solemnity: Is it right for women to assume positions of leadership, thereby usurping the authority God gave to men, and, Is it right for women to work?

We must make two observations before proceeding further. First, by tacking on that clause about usurping authority, we commit an informal fallacy of logic; we beg the question. If women in positions of authority are indeed usurping something, they are doing what they ought not do, and they are where they ought not be. Second, nobody objects to women *working;* the harder they work, the better men like it. The objection is that women work outside the home; they hold jobs when they should be keeping house, some contend.

In defense of Jane Byrne and Margaret Thatcher (and, of course, other women in positions of leadership), let it be said that they did not *seize* power. Therefore, it cannot be truthfully said that they are usurping authority granted to men. They were lawfully elected; in Chicago and in

Great Britain, more men vote than women. Thus, the women in question act as delegates. An analogy they might find amusing, but which, nonetheless, makes sense to people who want to live according to biblical principles, is the delegation of authority to women to serve in the Sunday school as choir leaders and the like. Bible students who reject the principle of delegated authority, as opposed to usurped authority, are stuck with the consequences, such as the need to fill every post with a male.

Biblical precedent defends women in positions of leadership. One thinks of Deborah, who presided over the affairs of the people of Israel about 1120 B.C. Some claim that she was an exception to the rule, and that the confused times in which she lived—when "everyone did what was right in his own eyes" (Judges 2:25)—account for her emergence as a leader (Judges 4:45). A legitimate response to these observations is that exceptions need not be limited to one; *if* there is a rule against women holding positions of leadership, one divinely approved exception admits the principle of exceptions. When circumstances demand them, there may be other exceptions as well.

Our own times are confused. Who is to say the times do not call for the rise of exceptional women who will do what a generation of "namby-pamby"men seems incapable of doing? In Britain, Margaret Thatcher was (and, of course, still is) known for her strong convictions about moral matters, and for her courage in expressing them. What have her male opponents been known for? Cynicism and political opportunism, according to Sir Harold Evans.[1] Britain—indeed *any* country—is better served by an intelligent woman with moral convictions than by the

---

[1]Sir Harold Evans, "Margaret Thatcher Rules Brittania," *Chicago Tribune*, 6 May 1979.

most consummate male politician, if he lacks conviction and courage.

It is possible that many Christian men who voted for Jane Byrne in Chicago, or Margaret Thatcher in Britain, agree that those women are exceptional, but contend that women in general should not seek either positions of leadership or employment outside the home. Take the question of outside employment. Titus 2 is usually cited in support of the position that it is unscriptural for women to get jobs. The passage contains instruction about the spiritual qualities men and women should exhibit and their respective roles in life. Older women are told to "encourage the young women to love their husbands, to love their children, to be sensible, pure, workers at home, kind, being subject to their own husbands, that the word of God may not be dishonored" (Titus 2:4-5). Did you catch the words, "workers [lit., "keepers"] at home"? This—being a worker at home—is said to be the role assigned to young women.

At least two observations are in order: First, Paul was thinking of young married women with children. Second, he was concerned about Christian testimony in the pagan world. If young mothers neglected their families, Paul suggests, the Word of God would be discredited. It was vital that the sanctity of marriage and the principle of genuine love be established as part of the Christian message. Many of my readers will agree that Paul's concerns are still valid. Young Christian mothers who neglect their families do a disservice to the cause of Christ.

Many Christians interpret the passage cited here as a command to young mothers to stay at home; they claim the passage forbids women to seek employment outside the home. In my judgment, such rigid interpretation of the passage is not necessary. Some mothers combine

17

outside interests with their work at home so efficiently that their husbands and children have no cause for complaint. These are inevitably restless, intelligent women for whom homemaking alone does not provide sufficient challenge or inner satisfaction. Have you noticed how many women who write powerful testimonies to contentment with their lot as housewives are professional writers? They stay at home, but keeping house is only part of their work. Much, if not most, of their energy is spent in writing, which is satisfying and, in many cases, becomes a lucrative career.

The restlessness of women who have no inclination for writing is understandable. Modern appliances have reduced the time and energy needed to keep house. Nobody spends all morning at the scrubbing board. Your handy Maytag takes care of the dirty clothes; you just dump them in and turn on the switch. Modern fabrics have almost eliminated the old drudgery of ironing shirts. The vacuum sweeper has replaced the old carpet beater. The list goes on. I know, of course, that "a woman's work is never done." Nevertheless, it *is* a whole lot easier than it used to be, and many women get bored at home. Their kids get on their nerves, especially on rainy days.

Before jumping all over women, let's consider two truths. First, not many *men* can keep the kids for a single day without feeling that their nerves have been stretched to the snapping point. Most men are wiped out in less than half a day of babysitting. Second, in Bible times—and even now in many lands—working at home did not mean that women were cooped up indoors all day, or that they did nothing but keep house. The division of labor was not as sharply divided as now, and the care of children was equitably, if not equally, divided among the adults. When the son of a prominent woman of Shunem (lit., a *great* woman) was old enough to work a bit, though still young enough to sit on his mother's lap, he went to the fields with his father (2 Kings 4:17-20).

Child-rearing in *all* its aspects was shared by both parents. Solomon remembered the instruction his father had given him. "When I was a son to my father," Solomon said, "Tender and the only son in the sight of my mother, then he taught me . . ." (Proverbs 4:4-5). On the other hand, King Lemuel remembered the oracle his mother taught him. If her words (see Proverbs 31) were autobiographical, Lemuel's mother was a very sharp woman who led a very rich life. She not only ran the royal household, but she purchased a field when it was needed. Her husband trusted her in everything. King Lemuel, remembering her, says that his mother "opens her mouth in wisdom, and the teaching of kindness is on her tongue" (Proverbs 31:26). Fathers and mothers shared responsibility for training the children.

Am I saying that all young mothers, or women of nearly any age, should get jobs outside the home? Not at all! I am just saying a word in support of women who, for any of several valid reasons, do get jobs. Some women *must* work; economic necessity forces them to seek gainful employment. They may be widows, or they may be married to men who either cannot or will not support their families. Among those who *cannot* are the disabled or sickly, or those whom the world calls unlucky. Their jobs never amount to anything, although they are thoroughly good men. Among those who *will not* support their families are the deliberately shiftless, those who spend their money on other women, and those who drink or gamble. Their wives *must* get jobs; staying at home is a luxury they cannot afford.

Some women must work for psychological reasons.

19

They yearn for careers outside the home, and because their grown or half-grown children are no longer completely dependent on them, they see no obstacle standing in the way of secular employment. Is this wrong? Motivation is an important factor in determining whether employment is the will of God for them, or a mistake to be avoided. If the objective is only money for fancier furniture, or some other "extra," then outside employment is probably wrong. It is certainly not worth its potential cost in such a case.

What is its potential cost? That depends on the woman. Bonnie G. Wheeler is rearing six children, three of whom are handicapped children whom she and her husband have adopted. They adopted the handicapped children, because the children needed loving parents. In an article titled, "Lessons from Alicia," Mrs. Wheeler tells what the family is learning from ten-year-old Alicia, who is deaf, mute, nearly blind, and functionally retarded, and has a congenital heart defect.[2] How many couples would adopt a child like Alicia? The Wheelers did, but they could not have adopted that child—or any of their afflicted children —if Bonnie Wheeler had been employed outside the home. For the Wheelers, no outside job could compensate for the loss of a home for those needy children.

Not many women are like Bonnie Wheeler. This is no adverse reflection on them; the Wheelers are most unusual. Some would say that their faith in taking those damaged children is a supernatural gift from the Holy Spirit (1 Corinthians 12:9). Whatever the explanation, it would be unreasonable to expect many women to imitate them—unless, of course, they also felt themselves yearn-

[2]See Bonnie G. Wheeler, "Lessons from Alicia," *Decision*, May 1979, p. 7.

ing for helpless children. Who knows? If Christian women were to open their hearts to the needs of the world's orphaned or flawed children, God might lead them to do what He has obviously led the Wheelers to do. For a woman conscious of the love of God flooding through her heart, bringing up orphaned or damaged children—especially those who have been rejected by their natural parents—would be a more satisfying career than pounding a typewriter in a downtown office.

There are other meaningful projects to occupy the minds and time of middle-class women who are bored with homemaking. (I say middle-class, because the wives of the poor seldom have any alternative to working outside the home.) The truth is, women who don't have to work could, if they would, undo some of the damage caused by the absences of women whose children really need them. Ideally, of course, children would be cared for by their own parents. In the real world, we have seen that this is not always possible. Even so, no child, whether small or nearly grown, needs to be left unattended. He should have the comfort and guidance of substitute mothers—unemployed women whose husbands earn enough to let them stay home and take care of the kids, and the kids of other parents.

Urban life in an industrialized nation brings problems peculiar to women in our times. In New Testament times, women went on having children until their middle years. There was always a baby coming, so that, when the children grew up and left the home, it was not left childless. Mother could still be a mother. But what do women in our generation do when the kids are gone? Having had only two or three—or at the most, four—children, a typical mother is left with nothing to do, before she is even fifty years old. Then what? Does she just sit around, watching soap operas and waiting for grandchildren?

The answer is plain: she finds something to do. What she does depends, of course, on various factors, including training and skills acquired through the years. The trouble is, many middle-aged mothers find themselves unprepared to do much of anything once their children leave the nest. For various reasons, they cannot adjust to mothering someone else's kids, and there are no jobs for women whose only skills are homemaking and raising children. Consequently, they have become a lost generation.

The church taught them to stay at home and bring up their kids. What does the church now propose to do with this lost generation of mothers without children?

3

Why Birth Control?

The topic of birth control was called to mind not too long ago by an article published by *Mother Jones*, exposing what it terms "a major occupational health scandal."[1] The scandal was sterility caused by a pesticide. Workers exposed to it, chiefly those who mixed the chemicals, were suffering from nosebleed, headaches, nausea, and, in some cases (actually all seven who were clinically tested), sterility.

Why should an article on work-related sterility persuade me to write about birth control? Because of two statements: first, an industry spokesman is quoted as saying (in a letter to the Occupational Safety and Health Administration), "While involuntary sterility caused by a manufactured chemical may be bad, it is not necessarily so. After all, there are many people now paying to have themselves sterilized to assure that they will no longer be able to become parents."[2]

The second statement is by the author of the article cited: "The official inertia (with respect to sterility-causing

[1] Daniel Ben-Horin, "The Sterility Scandal," *Mother Jones*, May 1979, pp. 51-63.

[2] Ibid., p. 63.

pesticides) was no coincidence. There are veils behind veils where occupational health is concerned. Get behind them all, and you're not looking at occupational health anymore; you're confronting the basic values of our economy and our society."[3]

The first statement can be dismissed as a callous remark. If it had been uttered rather than written, it could be regarded as an off-the-top-of-his-head comment, and certainly not a serious statement. True, some men do ask for vasectomies; they don't want children. But, generally speaking, they are not the kind of men to be found in factories. Even if they were factory workers, they would resent *involuntary* sterilization as much as anyone else, especially if it resulted from nothing more important than the production of another pesticide.

The second statement raises questions about values. The author is outraged—justly, I think—by industry's apparent willingness to expose workers to unknown dangers and, in some cases, clearly recognized dangers as well, in its pursuit of profits. A documentary film on occupational hazards, called *Song of the Canary*, begins with the explanation that, in the past, coal miners carried caged canaries into the mines. If the canaries collapsed, then the miners knew that carbon monoxide gas was forming. "Today," the film's narrator says, "the workers themselves may have become canaries for other workers and for society as a whole."[4] In the author's view, society—or at least that part of society that "calls the shots"—values cash profits more than the welfare of the men who produce the wealth.

[3]Ibid., p. 51.
[4]Ibid.

That is a harsh judgment, and I suspect that the author is only partly right. But I am intrigued by his indignation at the thought of sterility among workers. Not that I disagree with him; I also am indignant. However, there is a certain irony in the problem of involuntary sterility in a society that is seemingly bent on limiting human reproduction to as few as possible. Zero Population Growth is the goal. Not only do we seem to have convinced ourselves that we should have no more babies than are needed to replace old folks who die; we are busy exporting this philosophy to as many people as are willing to accept it.

Nobody really knows what would happen if the world should reach the goal of Zero Growth. There is no likelihood that it will reach that goal in our lifetime, if ever; underdeveloped countries (i.e., those that are not industrialized) tend to view children as possessions to be prized, not as creatures whose needs deprive the parents of things and pleasures they would otherwise have. In short, the poor peasants of the world like children, and they like them for what they become—a source of strength and support in old age. Consciously or not, they view them biblically—as gifts from the Lord. Consequently, they will go on having children.

Here, however, in the United States, we have succeeded in limiting the size of our families. If my figures are correct, the average family numbers 3.8 members, including two parents. That works out to slightly less than two children in each family—a statistical possibility that translates into families of varying sizes, few of which are big, by the standards of the rest of the world. Some have one or two children, and others none at all. What this means, among other things, is that schools are closing for lack of students; industry that served the needs of children (e.g., manufacturers of cribs and diapers) is cutting back; and we are becoming a nation of old people. The median age in the United States is considerably higher than elsewhere—with the exception of one or two western nations very much like us. In Africa, 50 percent of the people are under fifteen years of age.[5]

Several reasons can be given for the declining birth rate in the United States. Author Christopher Lasch draws attention to the "socialization of reproduction."[6] Says Lasch,

> In the course of bringing culture to the masses, the advertising industry, the mass media, the health and welfare services, and other agencies of mass tuition, took over many of the socializing functions of the home and brought the ones that remained under the direction of modern science and technology.[7]

What this amounts to is the weakening of the importance of the family. Does anyone seriously doubt the connection between the weakening of the family and the falling birth rate?

Even more significant is the narcissism of this generation. Narcissism is not a new word; psychologists have used it for a long time to indicate love of the body. The word derives from a legend of a Greek youth who fell in

[5]Basil Davidson, *Let Freedom Come: Africa in Modern History* (Norton, N.Y.: Little, 1978), p. 16.

[6]Christopher Lasch, *The Culture of Narcissism: American Life in an Age of Diminishing Expectations* (New York: Norton, 1978), p. 154.

[7]Ibid.

love with his own image, which he saw reflected in a pond, and pined away until he was transformed into a narcissus. In recent years, the word has been given wider circulation to indicate the ethos of those about whom Tom Wolfe writes in an article titled "The 'Me' Decade."[8]

I have on my desk a book titled *The Culture of Narcissism*. Its author defines a narcissist as one who, among other things, "demands immediate gratification and lives in a state of restless, perpetually unsatisfied desire. . . . [he] has no interest in the future because, in part, he has so little interest in the past."[9] In short, narcissism is a fancy word for egocentric selfishness.

Egocentric, selfish people don't want many children, if any at all. Why not? Because children make work; they sometimes cause grief; and they can be ruinously expensive, at least from the point of view of those parents who would rather spend their money on themselves. Narcissists don't view children biblically—that is, as gifts from the Lord. They resent them as intruders, or as unwanted "accidents," which resulted from the failure of a contraceptive device. Not until it is too late do couples who severely restrict the number of children they bring into the world become aware of the penalties their attitude lays upon them.

Meanwhile, Christian couples (in particular, those young enough to bring up children) should ask themselves whether they have blindly accepted the prevailing notions about the meaning of marriage and, of course, the bringing of children into the world, or have sought to know the

[8]Tom Wolfe, "The 'Me' Decade," *Harpers*, October 1975.
[9]Lasch, p. xvi.

mind of God, as revealed in the Bible. The Bible doesn't tell anybody how many children to have, but it does say enough about the purpose of marriage to enable a prayerful couple to formulate a few convictions about the subject. Consequently, the size of a family will not be determined by self-interest (using that word in its bad sense), but according to the couple's understanding of marriage according to the Bible.

What *is* marriage, according to the Bible? Theologian John Warwick Montgomery, citing Ephesians 5:22-32, makes three statements about marriage. First, it is *not* just a "procreative function." God did not design marriage *merely* to keep the race going. Second, marriage is *not* an end in itself. If it were, it would be maintained in eternity. The Bible says that "those who are considered worthy to attain to . . . the resurrection from the dead, neither marry, nor are given in marriage" (Luke 20:35). Third, Montgomery interprets the Ephesians passage to state that marriage "is seen as an *analogy*—indeed, the best human analogy—of the relationship between Christ and His Church."[10]

If marriage is an analogy of Christ's relationship with the church, then it follows that children are important to a marriage. Montgomery points to the connection between Christ's suffering and His "bringing many sons to glory."[11] Says Dr. Montgomery, "As the union of Christ and His Church does not exist for its own sake but to bring others to spiritual rebirth, so the marital reunion is properly

[10]John Warwick Montgomery, "How to Decide the Birth Control Question," *Birth Control and the Christian* (Wheaton, Ill.: Tyndale, 1969), p. 581.

[11]Ibid., p. 582; cf. Hebrews 2:10.

fulfilled in natural birth." What this means, says Montgomery, is that "to the extent possible and desirable, all Christian couples should seek to 'bring many sons to glory.' "[12]

This is not to say that Christian couples must have as many babies as can be conceived in a lifetime, or that birth control is improper. A few years ago, twenty-five evangelicals, all authorities in their respective fields of theology, medicine, genetics, law, and sociology, prepared an affirmation on birth control, in which they contended that "The prevention of conception is not in itself forbidden or sinful providing the reasons for it are in harmony with the total revelation of God for married life."[13] In my judgment, that position is in keeping with Scripture.

The question arises: how many children should a couple have? There is no universal answer. The twenty-five authorities already quoted list "disease, psychological debility, the number of children already in the family, and financial capability" as "factors determining whether pregnancy should be prevented."[14]

Montgomery says that married couples are "to consider it personally and prayerfully in light of their own physical, emotional, financial, and spiritual situation, and in light of the population picture in their area of the world."[15]

The trouble is, many Christian couples fail to seek an answer prayerfully; they do not consider the question in

[12]Ibid.

[13]Ibid., p. xxv.

[14]Ibid.

[15]Ibid., p. 583.

the light of biblical teaching on marriage as an analogy of Christ's relationship with the church. In addition, they seem to lack a truly Christian view of finances. Hence, many healthy, relatively prosperous couples either refuse to have children or restrict the number to one or two. They may live to regret it.

Refusal to have children carries certain consequences. The most obvious is loneliness in old age, and, of course, want of the support that one's grown children can provide. The same psalm that says that children are "a gift from the LORD" says that the children of one's youth are (in one's old age) "like arrows in the hand of a warrior" (Psalm 127:3-4). They provide a certain amount of protection. They also bring two special kinds of joy: the joy that belongs to parents whose children honor them in their old age, and the joy of having loving grandchildren. "Grandchildren," Solomon says, "are the crown of old men" (Proverbs 17:6).

Loneliness in old age is a terrible price to pay for refusal to have children in one's youth. (I realize, of course, that childlessness does not always come by choice. However, some couples choose to be childless, or to have only one or two children. It is to those whose childlessness is a conscious choice that I am speaking.) Refusal to have children may cost a man and wife the valuable lessons that only the discipline of rearing children can teach. One of these lessons is selfless tenderness. Nowhere is this more beautifully illustrated than in Jacob's encounter with Esau. When Esau proposed that they journey together, Jacob declined. "The children are frail . . ." he said. "I will proceed at my leisure . . . according to the pace of the children" (Genesis 33:13-14).

Nobody seriously urges a return to the days when women bore children every year until they were no longer able to do so. But there must be a happy medium between a house full of children and one with hardly any at all. If it can be found, it may be just the antidote needed for the narcissism of our age of self-indulgence.

4

An Ex-Abortionist on Abortion

Some time ago I saw an article titled "Fetal Transplants Could Resolve Abortion Conflict," and I said to myself, "Says who?"[1] In its *Roe vs. Wade* decision, handed down in 1973, the United States Supreme Court thought it was resolving the conflict over abortion, once and for all. Since then, scarcely a week has passed without the publication somewhere of an article criticizing that decision, or a report of conflict between pro-abortion and anti-abortion people. Millions of Americans (myself included) believe that the court's thinking was muddleheaded, and its decision wrong. As long as upwards of one million women and girls are aborting pregnancies every year in American clinics and hospitals, the controversy will remain unresolved.

I have at hand several recent articles, along with three impressive books—one hot off the presses. The book, *Aborting America*, is written by Bernard N. Nathanson, M.D., former director of the world's largest abortion clinic, located in New York City.[2] Dr. Nathanson

[1]Robert J. McClory, "Fetal Transplants Could Resolve Abortion Conflict," *The National Catholic Reporter*, 26 October 1979, pp. 1, 5.

[2]Bernard N. Nathanson with Richard N. Ostling, *Aborting America* (Garden City, N.Y.: Doubleday, 1979).

33

is an atheist; he does not believe in the existence of a personal God.[3] Nevertheless, after (or *while*) supervising the aborting of sixty thousand pregnancies, he changed his mind about abortion. Says Dr. Nathanson, "I have reached my conclusions very reluctantly, after six years of self-examination, but that makes the conclusions no less certain. On the contrary, it makes them more certain." Then he makes a curious statement: "Let me state once again that this is a humanistic philosophy drawn from modern biological data, not from religious creeds."[4]

Why is that statement curious? For two reasons: first, it underlines Dr. Nathanson's concern, lest he be confused with anti-abortion people whose conclusions coincide with his. Second, anti-abortionists, most of whom are religious, are unaccustomed to help from science or humanism. It would not occur to some of us that a humanist, working from different presuppositions, could reach the same conclusion as a Christian in so vital an issue as abortion.

The explanation may be ignorance; we don't read widely enough to know what others are saying about the subject. How many of us have read Baruch Brody's book, *Abortion and the Sanctity of Human Life: A Philosophical Enquiry*? Dr. Brody, Chairman of the Department of Philosophy at Rice University, is a Jewish scholar who makes a secular case against abortion.[5] Don't misunderstand me; I am not chiding you for not having read

[3]Ibid., p. 176.

[4]Ibid., p. 259.

[5]Baruch Brody, *Abortion and the Sanctity of Human Life: A Philosophical Enquiry* (Cambridge, Mass.: Massachusetts Institute of Technology, 1975).

Brody's book. I myself didn't even know of its existence before reading *Death Before Birth,* by Harold O. J. Brown.[6] Books such as *Death Before Birth* and *Handbook on Abortion*[7] present a biblical perspective—which is all we Christians need to know.

Nevertheless, we welcome the contributions of non-Christians such as Baruch Brody and Bernard Nathanson. Dr. Nathanson, in particular, brings to the subject the insights of an experienced abortionist, who "very reluctantly, after six years of self-examination," and, of course, serious thinking about abortion itself, wound up "agreeing with the Right-to-Lifers at many points."[8] Nathanson does not want to be identified with Right-to-Life supporters or any other anti-abortion group whose objections are essentially religious. His conclusions, he claims, were reached "wholly independently, based on [his] extensive experience in abortion."[9] By implication, Right-to-Lifers are not independent thinkers; they are captives of a religious creed.

At a recent conference held at Notre Dame University, Dr. Judith Blake, a UCLA sociologist and outspoken advocate of abortion-on-demand, produced a study purporting to show that opponents of abortion-on-demand are mainly "Catholics, Baptists, and other fundamentalist Protestants who attend church services regularly." Catholics and Protestants who don't attend church regularly are

[6]Harold O. J. Brown, *Death Before Birth* (New York: Thomas Nelson, 1977).

[7]Dr. and Mrs. J. C. Wilke, *Handbook on Abortion* (Cincinnati: Hiltz, 1971).

[8]Nathanson, p. 259.

[9]Ibid.

evidently indifferent to the subject.[10] The reaction of some in the audience, asking why Dr. Blake did not also cite the peculiarities of pro-abortionists, suggests that the religious factor was presented as if religious conviction were somehow disqualifying, as if being Catholic or Baptist or some other kind of fundamentalist fitted one only for programmed responses.

At least two comments are appropriate here: first, the charge that religion programs a person is a sword that cuts two ways. It can be said with just as much accuracy that a lack of religious conviction is seriously disqualifying; irreligious people lack a spiritual dimension to their thinking, without which their responses to moral issues are equally as predictable as those of religious people. Second, religious conviction (including a firm belief that the Bible is God's Word and, therefore, authoritative in matters of faith and practice) is better than conviction based on experience. Having performed many abortions, Dr. Nathanson no doubt *feels* much more strongly about his painfully reached conclusions than do the inexperienced. But why should it have been necessary for him (or any other doctor) to have learned the hard way (sixty thousand abortions and six years of self-examination) what religious people learn less destructively through Bible study? Who, in the final analysis, is captive—a Bible student who, knowing what the Bible teaches, recoils from abortion-on-demand, or a humanist who has to supervise sixty thousand deaths before reaching the Bible student's conclusions?

Aborting America is a useful book. Among its uses is its valid criticism of specious arguments on both sides of the question. Dr. Nathanson objects, among other things, to

[10]Quoted by McClory, p. 1.

terminology used by both camps. For example, he protests that terms such as "pro-life" and "Right-to-Life" are misleading, since those who go by these designations are not in favor of all life under all circumstances. Many so-called "pro-lifers" are also in favor of capital punishment.

"Pro-choice," on the other hand, is—in Dr. Nathanson's words—the "Madison Avenue euphemism of the other side."[11] "Pro-choice" means support for abortion-on-demand, and nothing else. Then why not say so plainly?   R. Emmett Tyrrell, Jr. explains:

> Most of the major ideas of our time are pish-posh, and most of the public thinkers of the day devote themselves to the decidedly distasteful exercise of disguising these ideas as creditable and at one with American constitutional process. When does the proponent of abortion admit to being pro-abortion? Perhaps in the wee hours and after many jugs have been passed. Otherwise, the advocate of abortion is always "pro-choice."[12]

A NARAL Report, titled "Violence Against the Right to Choose," illustrates this point.[13] The report rightly deplores the activities of "anti-choice fanatics" who burn abortion clinics. Since I said "*rightly* deplores," you know that I am not defending groups of individuals who fire-bomb abortion clinics. I merely draw attention to the misuse of language. The people who try to burn down abortion clinics may be fanatics, but they are not "*anti-*

[11]Nathanson, p. 171.

[12]R. Emmett Tyrrell, Jr., *The American Spectator*, December 1979.

[13]"Violence Against the Right to Choose," National Association for the Repeal of Abortion Laws, undated.

choice" fanatics; they oppose only one kind of choice—abortion-on-demand.

Dr. Nathanson may himself be guilty of misuse of language. He calls the unborn entity in the womb an "alpha." Why? It is a neutral term, he thinks. He rejects the term "fetus," because it is technically vague, and because it is used sarcastically by pro-abortionists who jeer at their opponents for being "friends of the fetus." Other clinical terms (e.g., conceptus, products of conception) are also unsatisfactory.

In Nathanson's view, terms such as "baby" and "unborn child" are also inappropriate, because those terms are customarily used for already-born infants. To apply "baby" or "unborn child" to the unborn entity still in the womb is to claim for that entity a type of life Dr. Nathanson is not willing to grant it. We Christians *are* willing to assign to the unborn entity in the womb the same kind of life characteristic of the already born, though under vastly different circumstances. A woman six months pregnant pats her tummy and thinks about her baby, not just her fetus or tissue. A Bible student reads the 139th psalm or the first chapter of Jeremiah and thinks of a person, not a "conceptus," a "fetus," or an "alpha."

God told Jeremiah that, before He formed him in the womb, He (God) knew him. The developing conceptus or fetus or alpha (choose any term you like) was a *person* at all stages of his development. Similarly, David's description of his development in the womb uses personal pronouns:

> For Thou didst form *my* inward parts; Thou didst weave *me* in *my* mother's womb. I will give thanks to Thee, for *I* am fearfully and wonderfully made . . . *My* frame was not hidden from Thee, when *I* was made in secret, and skillfully

wrought in the depths of the earth. Thine eyes have seen *my* unformed substance; and in Thy book they were all written, the days that were ordained for *me*, when as yet there was not one of them (Psalm 139:13-16, italics added).

Nobody knows whether unborn babies have self-consciousness, or whether they are aware of their murky surroundings, but the Scriptures leave no doubt about the *nature* of the life growing in the womb: it is human life—with all that humanness entails. The thing in the womb is a human being, a person, being readied for entrance into a world of human beings like him, yet uniquely different.

This is essentially Dr. Nathanson's view—unless I misunderstand him. He admits that alpha—his designation for the unborn entity in the womb—is human life, and that, from the moment of implantation of the blastocyst in the wall of the uterus, it is "an independent organism distinct from the mother."[14] He also says that all that happens at birth is that "the organism is put into a different physiological milieu, and nothing more. It is like switching from AC to DC current; the energy connection changes, but the basic mechanics remain the same."[15]

This point is crucial to Nathanson's thinking; it renders invalid many of the arguments used by pro-abortion people. Says Nathanson,

> I am reluctantly led to agree with Paul Ramsay that every good argument for abortion is a good argument for infanticide. Obstetricians above all would have to agree that birth constitutes no dramatic shift in dependency, status, or

[14]Nathanson, p. 216; cf. pp. 196-97, 207.

[15]Ibid., p. 211.

function. Once we see this line for what it is, there is no remaining distinction between a dependent non-viable alpha and a viable one, or between a viable alpha within the womb and a newborn outside it.[16]

Dr. Nathanson believes that fact, once it is widely understood, will lead to infanticide in America. Already, some fairly well-known philosophers openly advocate infanticide. Nathanson cites one who thinks that newborn humans have no more self-consciousness than kittens and, therefore, should be given a week after birth for observation, with survival or extinction the issue to be decided.[17]

What kind of people contend for such a position? They may be quite pleasant; they are certainly intellectually honest. Rejecting specious arguments in support of the position they favor (i.e., abortion-on-demand), they develop the only argument that can be used to justify it (i.e., that an unborn human life is *not a person*), and they carry it to its *logical conclusion*—that a newborn baby is *not a person*, and, under some circumstances, can be put to death. One published philosopher does not object to infanticide on principle, but opposes it on practical grounds, because "most people value infants."[18]

Among other things, this illustrates the biblical proverb that "bad company corrupts good morals" (1 Corinthians 15:33). Only God and, perhaps, thoughtful historians know what can happen to a society that denies personhood to unborn and newborn babies. If personhood—defined by these philosophers in terms of consciousness, self-awareness, reasoning, and such—is not inherent in

[16]Ibid., pp. 225-26.
[17]Ibid., p. 224.
[18]Ibid.

biological life, if it is acquired at a late stage in fetal development, or even after birth itself, who is to say that it may not be lost? Are comatose patients non-persons? If so, what shall we do with them? You see where this line of reasoning can take you.

Dr. Nathanson is right in objecting to the notion that personhood and human life are separable. Says he,

> Personhood does not really depend upon consciousness, but upon people recognizing the human life that is there among us, beyond this strange talk of "human beings" who are not yet "persons," beyond the word games and the straw men, beyond the guppies and the kittens, beyond the labels that writers devise to camouflage their point system for assigning value to human lives, and beyond an insubstantial utilitarian ethic that fails to come up to the lowest levels of human justice.[19]

Right on, Dr. Nathanson! You may not like it, but your thinking is almost biblical.

[19]Ibid., p. 226.

5

For Homosexuals

What I have to say is my response to a telephone call from one homosexual and an unsigned letter from another. Not long ago, I got a call from a man who said he worked for a newspaper published for homosexuals. He wanted to know if I thought homosexuals should be put to death. The question startled me. I confessed that it had not occurred to me that anybody would recommend the death penalty for homosexual practices. He assured me that spokesmen for anti-gay groups had indeed called for capital punishment of practicing homosexuals. In proof of this, he sent me copies of reports carried in *The Chicago Tribune*. Sure enough, a man who probably expressed only a personal opinion—not the views of any organization—was quoted as linking homosexuality with "murder and other sins" deserving the death penalty.[1]

This makes many Christians uneasy. Why? Because the Bible does not single out homosexual practice as worthy of death, to the exclusion of other sins. I do not minimize the seriousness of homosexual practices. However, homosexuals aren't the only offenders whose practices will keep them out of the kingdom of God. According to Paul, "Neither the sexually immoral nor idolaters nor male

[1] See "Anti-Gay Ad Blitz Planned," *Chicago Tribune*, 11 February 1981; "Majority Rule," *Chicago Tribune*, 16 February 1981.

prostitutes nor homosexual offenders nor thieves nor the greedy nor drunkards nor slanderers . . . will inherit the kingdom of God" (1 Corinthians 6:9-10, NIV*).

Jesus said that "from within, out of men's hearts, come evil thoughts, sexual immorality, theft, murder, adultery, greed, malice, deceit, lewdness, envy, slander, arrogance and folly" (Mark 7:21-22, NIV). In a short list of types destined for the lake of fire, John includes "the cowardly, the unbelieving, the vile, the murderers, the sexually immoral, those who practice magic arts, the idolaters and all liars" (Revelation 21:8). A few paragraphs later, John adds to this list those he terms "the dogs" (probably male prostitutes), and anyone who adds to or takes away from his prophecy (Revelation 22:15, 18-19).

There's no comfort in any of these lists for practicing homosexuals. Where homosexuals are not specified, they are included in the category of "the sexually immoral." Homosexual practice is consistently condemned. However, my purpose in reading the lists is not to indict homosexuals or to take sides with those who call for their execution. Biblically speaking, adulterers, thieves, gossips, and slanderers are all in the same predicament as homosexual offenders. Consequently, it's a bold, confident man who would call for the execution of a single category of sinners.

This is not to say that practices that God condemns alike *as sin* are the same socially. Some sins are worse than others. Certainly the law distinguishes between murder and slander. A murderer destroys life, which cannot be recalled. A slanderer destroys reputations, which can be rebuilt. Hence, the law does not call for the execution (or even the imprisonment) of slanderers or libelers. They are

New International Version.

44

merely fined. What about homosexuals? Are homosexual sins as lethal as murder? The answer is *no*. True, homosexuals may recruit hitherto innocent partners and corrupt them. However, even recruitment (the fear of which is at the root of much hatred directed at homosexuals) is not as bad as murder. In the first place, the recruit is not entirely innocent; he cooperates with the man who seeks to corrupt him. Second, his plight is not hopeless. If he desires it, he can escape.

Can a homosexual change? I just said that he can, but is it true? A prior question now being asked in many places is, *Should* he change? A homosexual's friends tell him to accept himself as he is. Is it necessary to change, or are so-called "gay activists" right in defending their manner of life as a justifiable alternative? The question is now being asked in surprising places. In an article published in *Pastoral Renewal*, counselor Anthony Cassano relates efforts being made in Roman Catholic and evangelical circles to win acceptance of homosexuality. Says Cassano,"In less than a dozen years the orthodox position has been put on the defensive in Catholic theological circles and homosexual behavior has gained considerable tacit acceptance."[2]

Cassano warns evangelicals that "the parallels between the Catholic church and the evangelical movement are significant."[3] However, Cassano says,

The evangelical world has not yet grasped that there is a battle going on for Christian sexual morality, and has not yet joined forces to respond. As a consequence, there is the

[2]Anthony Cassano, "Coming Out in the Churches," *Pastoral Renewal*, March 1981, p. 72.

[3]Ibid.

likelihood that the evangelical movement will in the 1980's travel the same road the Catholic Church trod in the 1970's. It may end with condemnation of homosexual behavior by some evangelical leaders and acceptance by others.[4]

What does the Bible teach about homosexual practices? The same thing it teaches about adultery or any other kind of sexual immorality. Anthony Cassano summarizes it correctly:

> For the individual, the New Testament teaches that unrepented homosexual behavior results in exclusion from the kingdom of God. To those whose teaching leads others into sexual immorality, Scripture applies some of its severest condemnations. To the church which tolerates the teaching of sexual immorality, Scripture delivers stern rebukes.[5]

Those who answer that practicing homosexuals should not change, claiming to base their answer on Scripture, are guilty of wresting Scripture, which, as Peter warns, they do to their own destruction (2 Peter 3:16).

Can a homosexual change? Yes, if he turns to Christ—after which the designation "homosexual" is no longer suitable. Cassano urges such Christians not to think of themselves as homosexuals, but as Christians with a particular problem. If a man thinks he is a homosexual, he becomes "susceptible to gay propaganda about the kind of character, relationships, and lifestyle that must go along with homosexual desires."[6] If, however, he really wants to follow Christ, he can change.

[4]Ibid., pp. 72-73.

[5]Ibid., pp. 73-74.

[6]Anthony Cassano, "Christian Men and Homosexual Desires," *Pastoral Renewal*, April 1981, p. 76.

The first step is acceptance of biblical teaching about homosexuality. Instead of torturing the Word of God to make it approve homosexual relationships—or at least refrain from condemning them—a homosexual must accept the plain teaching of Scripture. He must admit that the Bible does not tolerate homosexual practices. Hence, if he claims the title of "Christian," he *must* change. As Paul says, in a statement as appropriate for homosexuals as for adulterers, "Everyone who confesses the name of the Lord must turn away from wickedness" (2 Timothy 2:19, NIV). If we claim to be Christians, we must abandon those practices that the Bible condemns as sinful.

The second essential step toward a changed life is a complete break with the so-called "gay community." This is the biblical doctrine of separation. Paul admonishes us not to be yoked together with unbelievers. He asks several rhetorical questions, designed to point out the inconsistency of fellowship among those as opposite as light and darkness. Listen to Paul's conclusion:

"Therefore, COME OUT FROM THEIR MIDST AND BE SEPARATE," says the Lord. "AND DO NOT TOUCH WHAT IS UNCLEAN: And I will welcome you. And I will be a father to you, and you shall be sons and daughters to Me," says the Lord Almighty (2 Corinthians 6:17-18; cf. Isaiah 52:11).

Did you hear it? The passage is an admonition to separation from evil and evil companions. It is also a promise: God Himself will receive us. This is His offer to men and women teetering between two ways of living. For Christians with homosexual desires, a complete break with the homosexual world means fellowship with the living God, who comes to us as a heavenly Father.

A *complete* break is crucial to change. Committed

homosexuals have a vested interest in preventing change. Every changed life weakens their contention that homosexuality is legitimate behavior. A break with Christian homosexual support groups is also necessary. The fatal weakness of these groups is that they are usually staffed by ex-homosexuals. These men are unreliable counselors. Why? Counseling by ex-homosexuals, says Anthony Cassano, ". . . places the men in proximity with those who would be the greatest source of temptation. . . . The possibility of mutual attraction among those with homosexual desires will often undermine the group."[7] Consequently, homosexuals who want to change should seek the help of heterosexual counselors.

Stanley R. Strong, in an article published in the *Journal of Psychology and Theology,* describes an effective counselor. He is a man to whom "the client is a beloved of God, one of God's prized children, and is a fellow traveler under the cross."[8] Says Strong, who believes that homosexuality is "a distortion of the core being of the client," the counselor "responds to the negative aspects of the client's behavior not in anger and condemnation, but in sorrow in the client's hurt and need of redemption." In this way, the counselor provides "a context of promise, renewal, and change to the homosexual," with a view to the homosexual client's "renewal as God's beloved who is being molded by the Holy Spirit into the likeness of Christ."[9]

[7]Ibid.

[8]Stanley R. Strong, "Christian Counseling with Homosexuals," *Journal of Psychology & Theology* 8, no. 4 (Winter 1980): 283-84.

[9]Ibid., p. 284.

Why do I quote Professor Strong here? Because I'd like to draw my letter-writing friend away from his homosexual acquaintances and lead him to a Christian counselor who can offer help toward his growth into the likeness of Christ. Sensible Christian counselors don't offer painless remedies; they don't promise an end to homosexual orientation in every case, although Professor Strong contends that, when homosexuals call on the Holy Spirit to enter their lives in power, "change occurs on two fronts, forgiveness and the healing of memories, and change in the overt sexual behavior and desires."[10]

A pamphlet titled "Homosexuality and the Miracle Makers" denies the possibility of change.[11] Yet change in behavior, if not in inner orientation, cannot be denied; as in Paul's day, there are too many living witnesses to the possibility of changed lives. Paul reminded his friends at Corinth that some of them *had been* sexually immoral. Some of them *had been* adulterers. Some *had been* homosexual offenders. But, said Paul, ". . . you were washed . . . you were sanctified . . . you were justified in the name of the Lord Jesus Christ, and in the Spirit of our God" (1 Corinthians 6:11).

Emphasis in the Bible is on changed lives. Paul does not say whether converted homosexuals become heterosexuals. He does not say whether they lose their homosexual tendencies. Why not? Possibly because he may not have considered the question important. What mattered was an end to sinful *practices*, whether homosexual or heterosexual. Homosexuals were commanded to stop the homosex-

[10]Ibid., p. 285.

[11]Jim Peron, "Homosexuality and the Miracle Makers," privately printed. Available from the author.

ual practices, and men and women living immorally were told to stop the fornication. Change in manner of life is—or is expected to be—immediate. Change in the inner world—the world of thought and reflection and fantasies—is progressive and takes longer. It may take a lifetime.

I suspect that homosexuals who are scornful of the possibility of change are disinclined to change. Possibly they dread the inner struggle such change entails, which the Bible does not conceal. Certainly much, if not most, secular literature on sexuality assumes the right to sexual "fulfillment." This plea is fundamental to attempts by gay-rights spokesmen to gain legal recognition of their manner of life. The Bible, on the other hand, does not support the right to *improper* satisfaction of any basic human drives. The sexual drive, the Bible teaches, may be satisfied only in marriage between a man and a woman.

Does this approach condemn men and women with homosexual tendencies to celibacy? Anthony Cassano objects to the word "celibacy." Says he,

> "Celibacy" demands a degree of asceticism to which few are called and for which most are not gifted. The more usual terms for refraining from immoral sexual activity would be "chastity" or "continence." It has always been expected that Christians who are temporarily or permanently unable to marry would practice chastity or continence. Expressed this way, the norm has not sounded like an intolerable burden.[12]

Whether we like it or not, God calls us to abstinence except within marriage. This forbids all homosexual activi-

[12]Cassano, "Coming Out," p. 72.

ty. It may be cold comfort to homosexuals that the ban includes the far more common sins of heterosexuals. But it's no comfort to anybody that, because of these things— *all* of these sexual excesses so popular in our times—"the wrath of God comes upon the sons of disobedience" (Ephesians 5:6).

6

Should Christians Drink?

What I have to say is directed primarily to Christians who are tempted to drink. You already know my point of view; the word "tempted" gives it away. I believe that, for Christians, even moderate drinking is wrong, and I'd like to tell you why.

First, let me admit that the distinction between Christians and non-Christians is somewhat misleading. If there are moral—not merely legalistic—reasons for abstaining, they are equally valid for Christians and non-Christians. The notion that God does not hold a non-Christian accountable for what he does is not biblical. Paul says, "Let no one deceive you with empty words, for because of these [evil] things, the wrath of God comes upon the sons of disobedience" (Ephesians 5:6). Consequently, I urge you who are not Christians to read on as well. You may discover something useful.

Is moderate drinking by Christians an issue? No pastor doubts it. Social drinking is increasing among Christians, with the same inevitable effects it has elsewhere, including alcoholism. True, we don't see as much alcoholism among Christians as among non-Christians; it is not as visible. Drinkers drop out; they seldom appear in church. One suspects, however, that the percentages are comparable. That is, proportionately, as many Christians as non-

Christians who begin drinking socially become alcoholics. *The law of reaping and sowing operates without regard to race or religion.*

Why do professing Christians drink? For nearly as many reasons as do non-Christians, including a subtle belief that gracious living demands it. Distillers tell us this constantly. In a study of changing drinking habits in the United States, *Fortune* notes that a leading manufacturer of vodka aims its ads at "leisure-time consumption—aboard the boat, off the tennis court, on the front-porch swing where the drinker and her boyfriend used to sip lemonade when they were kids." The people in the ads are inevitably attractive; they "exemplify drinkers who weave the use of alcohol into moderate and relaxed life-styles."[1] Only a slob doesn't know the difference between a chablis and a rosé, and when to serve them.

The mind-benders are hugely successful; vast hordes of people now believe that alcohol is essential to gracious living, notwithstanding the clearly visible damage that is being done. For Christians, there is less excuse than for others. We are warned *in advance* not to listen to every spirit that whispers ever so seductively. As Paul says, "Don't let the world around you squeeze you into its own mould, but let God re-make you so that your whole attitude of mind is changed. Thus you will prove in practice that the will of God is good, acceptable to him and perfect" (Romans 12:2, Phillips*). We are not called to "gracious living"— as the world fancies it.

Christians who drink expose themselves to alcoholism, even as unbelievers do. Is the risk serious? Yes, it is. I

---

[1]Charles G. Burck, "Changing Habits in American Drinking," *Fortune*, October 1976, p. 158.

*J. B. Phillips, *The New Testament in Modern English*.

have before me an article published in a newsmagazine not long ago, titled "Women Alcoholics." Ironically, the article was featured in the "Life/Style" section. Some life! Some style! The women are drunks who, beguiled into drinking by the thought that a couple of drinks would make them feel "warm, compassionate, loving, considerate, expressive, open, pretty, affectionate, and sexy," quickly became alcoholics. In women, the disease—as alcoholism is now defined—develops faster than in men. The article says "there is evidence that women's livers are more damaged by liquor than men's." Furthermore, research shows a connection between heavy drinking and gynecological problems, including the possibilities of abnormalities in children born to women who drink during pregnancy.[2]

The social effects are nearly as devastating. Alcoholic women are "pariahs," or outcasts. Their husbands leave them; their families deny them treatment; and the women go on drinking alone. None of them expected to become an alcoholic; each of them began quite innocently.

In the case of Christians, the case may not be quite so innocent; we should know better. True, when the question is raised, someone in the crowd usually says that Paul urged Timothy to take a little wine for his stomach's sake (1 Timothy 5:23). That settles the matter for some. Certainly wine's medicinal properties were important in ancient times, before man discovered Alka-Seltzer. Wine was also used externally as a disinfectant. The Good Samaritan poured oil and wine on the wounds of the man who had been mugged on the road to Jericho (Luke 10:33-34).

[2]Susan Cheever Cowley, "Women Alcoholics," *Newsweek*, 15 November 1976, p. 73.

Nevertheless, I am unable to believe that a prescription for one man's digestive disorders is apostolic permission to drink; nor am I convinced that wine is purely medicinal. In the absence of something better, it may be the thing for indigestion and skin abrasions, but for certain maladies, it is unquestionably toxic. In any case, the Bible has far less to say about its potentially beneficial properties than about its misuse, and the resultant evils.

For example, the first mention of strong drink in the Bible is found in Genesis; Noah got drunk on homemade wine and lay in his tent (Genesis 9:21). This was evidently a great disgrace. Everyone knows that Noah was having a hangover when he cursed Canaan (Genesis 9:24-25).

Not long after that scene we find the description of Lot's drunkenness. In his befuddled state, he became a contributor to the incestuous conception of both Moab and Ammon—progenitors in turn of Israel's traditional enemies (Genesis 19:30-38).

Between those two references to the misuse of drink, we read of that incredibly beautiful meeting of Abraham and Melchizedek. The mysterious king of Salem met Abraham, who was slogging wearily home after the battle with the marauding kings of the east. Melchizedek gave Abraham a meal of bread and wine (Genesis 14:18-20). Obviously, this was a very different use of wine than that of Noah and Lot. But their misuse of it was probably typical of many who drank in Old Testament days. Certainly the Bible contains more references to drunkenness than to the genteel sipping of wine at meals.

Neither Noah nor Lot could be described as social drinkers, to be sure. They drank alone; in neither instance was there that conviviality that is supposed to make drinking fun. The Bible tells of social drinking, however—parties that began innocently but ended in disaster. The case of the Levite in Judges 19 can hardly be beaten for horror. While riffraff abused his wife outside, all was warm and cheery inside, and the Levite's heart was merry, as he drank with his new friends. If he had stayed sober, he might have heard his wife's screams in time to save her.

Second Samuel 13:29 tells of the plot by which Amnon was murdered. Absalom commanded his men to strike Amnon when his heart was "merry with wine," so that he could not defend himself.

Some may protest that this is beside the point. They will agree wholeheartedly that drunkenness is sin; it would never occur to them to defend it. They distinguish clearly between moderate drinking of alcoholic beverages and drunkenness, and, admittedly, it is a valid distinction. A believer who drinks a little wine or takes a cocktail is not necessarily a sinner on that account. He may have his reasons for doing it. However, in checking every reference in the Bible to strong drink, I am left with a conviction that alcohol destroys far more often than it heals, and the use of it tends to misuse.

That last statement is worth repeating: *use of it tends to misuse*. That is the evidence of Scripture (for all who believe the Holy Spirit had a reason for recording drunken scenes), and it is certainly the evidence of contemporary life. Drunkenness in America is on the increase, as everybody knows. This doesn't mean that the nation's drunks get drunk more frequently than in the past; it means that there are more drunks. More people than ever before in our history are now drinking and getting drunk, and more and more of them are becoming alcoholics. The article on "Women Alcoholics" is a frightening piece of evidence.

Nobody really knows why some do become addicted to

alcohol and others do not. But the testimony of many alcoholics is that they were hooked by the first drink. According to literature produced by many alcohol research organizations, including the National Institute on Alcohol and Drug Abuse (created by Congress in 1970), chronic drunkenness is caused by "varying combinations of psychological, physiological, and environmental factors."[3] The diagnosis is remarkable for its lack of precision. Yet its very vagueness underlines the fact that addiction to alcohol is unpredictable. Certain men and women become alcoholics, while members of the same families who have more or less the same genetic make-up do not succumb.

In my thinking, this fact—that addiction is unpredictable—is all the reason any Christian needs for avoiding the first drink. As Paul declared to the Corinthian believers, "All things are lawful for me, but not all things are profitable. All things are lawful for me, but I will not be mastered by anything" (1 Corinthians 6:12).

Dr. G. Aiken Taylor, who has spent a lot of time and energy studying the effects of alcohol, makes this point nicely. Says he, "every single one of the millions who is addicted to alcohol began his voyage to the hell of addiction with a first sip." A nationally syndicated column on the dangers of abuse has urged that "Youngsters must be persuaded to desist when there is any indication that their drinking is leading to trouble." Dr. Taylor deplores this advice. Why? Because by then it is too late; the youthful drinker is already hooked.[4]

What shall we say about the oft-repeated assertion that

---

[3] *The National Observer*, 2 October 1971.

[4] G. Aiken Taylor, "What About the Deadliest of Them All?" *Christianity Today*, 7 June 1974.

Jesus drank wine with His meals? This was perhaps the only charge of personal depravity brought against Him. "A gluttonous man and a winebibber," His enemies said. The charges were scurrilous and false, as every believer knows; Jesus was neither glutton nor drunkard. Yet He may have taken wine with His meals, and we have found no evidence that He ever commanded His disciples to abstain. This, combined with the fact that there is not unmistakable biblical prohibition against the use of alcohol, leads some Christians to think that a permissive attitude is in order.

This is probably an oversimplification of scriptural teaching on the subject. There are good reasons for believing that abstinence in these times, at least in this land, would have the support of Scripture. Certainly circumstances are different here from those that prevailed in Bible times. Would anyone *seriously* argue that wine is indispensable for medicinal purposes, or that it is safer than our municipal water supplies, or that Christ would ask for the wine list in a restaurant?

Dr. Taylor believes that arguments favoring permissiveness toward the use of alcohol closely resemble those formerly used to support slavery. Says he,

> It *can* be shown that the Bible tolerates slavery. . . . But the Church long ago concluded that slavery violates personhood designed to be conformed to the image of God's Son. By the same token, even though one cannot find in Scripture a polemic against the use of beverage alcohol, the overwhelming evidence suggests that alcohol should be shunned.[5]

The effect of alcohol on those prone to addiction, along

[5]Ibid.

with the consequences of those who regard it with horror provide one good reason for shunning it.

The apostle Paul felt strongly that we must respect another man's conscience. It is astonishing how much space he devoted to the question of making adjustments in one's life-style out of consideration for a brother with scruples about certain matters. In some cases, the scruples (viewed from Paul's personal standpoint) were preposterous. Yet, reading Paul's letters, we become aware of the extraordinary lengths to which he would go to avoid giving his weaker brother occasion for stumbling. "For even Christ did not please Himself" (Romans 15:3), the apostle wrote. For him, that was final.

Finally, we must face the awful possibility of giving the first drink to a brother or sister in whom the "varying combinations of psychological, physiological, and environmental factors" that lead to alcohol addiction lie sleeping, waiting to be aroused. There may be many Christians carrying a burden of guilt for having done precisely that. Dr. Taylor suspects that "if all those who became addicted to alcohol after starting to drink in imitation of a professing Christian were gathered in one place, they would constitute a multitude."[6] It seems to me that it would be hard to live with guilt like that.

[6]Ibid.

7

Smoking—An Abnormal Habit

The source is an article published in *Science 80*. Here is a line from its closing paragraph: "Smoking a cigarette will never again be regarded as altogether normal behavior."[1]

I'm interested in smoking for two reasons: first, some of my good friends smoke, and, although not all of them are trying to stop, all (without exception) wish they had never begun. Second, people call me to ask if smoking is a sin. They smoke, but their consciences bother them, probably because they sense the disapproval of some of their Christian friends.

Smoking is no longer primarily a religious problem—if it ever was. It is now recognized as a health problem and, therefore, a social issue. Every pack of cigarettes carries a label saying, "The Surgeon General has determined that cigarette smoking is harmful to your health." No doubt you have noticed the cigarette industry's reluctance to admit the validity of the evidence against tobacco. The label reveals it. Instead of saying flatly, "Cigarette smoking is harmful to your health," the copy writers tell us that "The Surgeon General has determined . . .," thereby

[1]William Bennett, "The Cigarette Century," *Science 80*, September-October 1980.

suggesting that it's just one man's opinion. In my judgment, this is contemptible, though no more so than ads that attempt to convince you that smoking is *macho* or satisfying or definitely the "in" thing to do.

The fact that cigarette smoking is harmful to your health is so heavily documented that the issue is no longer debatable, except by people with axes to grind. The article cited earlier, titled "The Cigarette Century," by William Bennett, reviews some of the chemical and physiological data of importance to the discussion. Bennett says that about a hundred years ago (September 4, 1880), a twenty-year-old man named James Bonsack filed for a patent on his first invention—a cigarette-rolling machine. His invention made cheap cigarettes a possibility, and, recounts Bennett, "before long, a new type of tobacco made them a necessity for millions of people."[2] Cigarettes have become a necessity by virtue of the addictive power of the new tobacco. Within a short time, smokers get hooked; they cannot quit.

The new tobacco isn't really "new"; it's the flue curing method that makes it "new," as contrasted with the tobacco cured by the primitive methods prevailing before the Civil War. The flue method, perfected after the Civil War, produced milder tobacco, but it also "significantly altered the chemistry" of tobacco. It made the substance slightly acid instead of alkaline, and that made tobacco addictive. How?

Bennett explains:

Nicotine passes easily through living tissue only when it is in an alkaline medium. Under even slightly acid conditions,

[2]Ibid.

virtually every molecule of nicotine carries an electric charge that prevents it from crossing membranes. Pipe and cigar tobaccos, cured by age-old methods, yield an alkaline smoke, from which nicotine can be gradually absorbed in modest quantities through the mucous membranes of the mouth. The alkalinity itself makes the smoke irritating and deters inhalation. By contrast, the slight acidity of cigarette smoke is not readily absorbed if the smoke is just held in the mouth. But because cigarette smoke is not highly irritating, it can be drawn into the lungs—indeed, it must be for absorption to occur. On the lungs' vast surface the acidity is neutralized; the nicotine loses its electric charge and passes rapidly into the bloodstream. From the lungs, nicotine-loaded blood is carried back to the heart, which gives a squeeze and sends about 15 percent of the inhaled dose directly, and undiluted, to the brain. The brain, in turn, takes up on the first pass virtually all the nicotine carried to it. The whole journey takes seven seconds. In comparison, heroin injected into the forearm takes about 14 seconds to reach the brain, and on its way, the dose becomes diluted by blood from other parts of the body.[3]

Bennett goes on to discuss addiction. He says that conventional explanations of cigarette smoking have called it a psychological dependence "in which the child's pacifier and security blanket are rolled into one little white tube for grown-up use." Not so, says Bennett. There is evidence that pipe and cigar smoking may be explained in this way, but not cigarette smoking. Cigarettes are too hard to give up to be explained in terms of psychological dependency; they do not easily yield to other crutches. Smokers who try to quit suffer from both physical and psychological factors that persist, in some cases (about 20 percent) five to nine years. Bennett observes, "By now

[3]Ibid.

there is little doubt that the drug [nicotine], absorbed in the right way, creates a state of drug dependency."[4]

This brings us to so-called religious reasons for not smoking. Is it a sin to smoke? I think it is. However, let me reassure you, if you are a smoker: I do not wish to be offensive, nor do I wish to give the impression that smoking is in the same class as, say, the so-called "seven deadly sins," which include such failings as sloth, envy, and lust. Nevertheless, I am now more convinced than ever that our grandfathers who thought it was a sin to smoke were right. I grew up among Christians who shunned smoking. They shunned quite a few other cultural features of society around them as well—dancing, playing cards, going to the movies, and even bowling. In my youth, the scriptural basis for objection to these activities was not always (if ever) clearly presented, and we young people chafed under the restraints. Was the refusal to participate just evidence of our people's need of symbols capable of expressing their separation from the world around them?

I didn't know, but I felt then, as now, that smoking was certainly not in the class of sins alluded to already. The Bible does not say, "Thou shalt not smoke." The Bible does not specifically mention countless twentieth century activities which are nonetheless objectionable and, on the basis of general principles laid down in the Bible, should be avoided. Take the example of heroin. Where does it say, "Thou shalt not mainline heroin?" Yet no serious person would defend the habit from either a social or biblical perspective.

Two principles which, it seems to me, are applicable to

[4]Ibid.

smoking, are presented in a passage in which Paul replies to believers in Corinth who misunderstood the concept of Christian liberty. They, like many first century Christians (and twentieth century Christians), turned the grace of God into license."All things are lawful," Paul declares, "but not all things are profitable. All things are lawful, but not all things edify" (1 Corinthians 10:23).

What Paul means is clear: activities which may be technically permissible—because they are not specifically forbidden—may be prohibited on other grounds, such as their essential uselessness, potential for harm, or addicting power. These are two valid objections to smoking, and I recall hearing them often in my youth. "I will not be brought under the power of any," our preachers thundered, with that fierce intensity of men who know what they believe and don't care if the whole world disagrees with them. They believed, as I do, that smoking cigarettes was not merely useless; it was wasteful and harmful *and* addictive—the addiction itself is sufficient reason for refusing to smoke. To be *unable* to quit? To be *in bondage* to a smelly, costly habit? To be *mastered* by anything but Christ?

Our preachers thought and talked pictorially; they likened smokers to belching chimneys and roared that they were burning up money which belonged to the Lord and should have been used with a sense of trusteeship, or stewardship. Most of us (certainly I speak for myself) are too vulnerable in this area to say much. Smokers do waste money; they literally burn it up. But we non-smokers waste money too. God alone knows how much we waste—and where we waste it.

That, of course, is no argument in favor of smoking. It's no more valid than the charge, heard to the point of weariness, that coffee and tea are also addictive. Does anybody really believe that? Coffee and tea may be habit-forming, and mounting evidence indicates that the caffeine in coffee has adverse effects on the health of *some* coffee drinkers. But no authorities believe that coffee and tea are in the same class as cigarettes. In any case, the alleged addiction of coffee and tea drinkers does not justify addiction to nicotine.

Earlier, we saw what happens when nicotine is inhaled; from the lungs it passes into the bloodstream via the heart. We no longer doubt what this does to the body. In a separate article, titled "Paying the Piper," William Bennett talks about the damage done by nicotine poisoning. Says he, "The evidence that cigarettes shorten life is overwhelming." Everybody is now aware of the link between cigarettes and cancer. "But the cancer connection," Bennett contends,

> is not the major cause of death in smokers. Rather, it is coronary heart disease. Second comes lung cancer. General deterioration of the lung tissue is third. After these three major causes, a variety of other diseases and cancers make a further contribution to the high death rate of smokers. Cancers of the larynx, mouth, esophagus, bladder, kidney, and pancreas are all more common in smokers than non-smokers. So are ulcers of the stomach and intestine, which are more likely to be fatal in smokers. Women who smoke during pregnancy run a significant risk that their babies will die before or at birth. The newborns are likely to weigh less, to arrive prematurely, and to be more susceptible to "sudden infant death."[5]

In light of these facts, one is mystified by the apparent unwillingness of smokers to quit and the rush by adolescents to begin smoking.

[5]William Bennett, "Paying the Piper," *Science 80*, n.d.

No doubt the explanation is that most smokers would like to quit but can't; they're hooked by a powerful addiction. Yet to all outward appearances, they *seem* not to be hooked; they *seem* to enjoy their smokes, despite the damage that is being done inside their bodies. The image they project, greatly enhanced, of course, by the advertising industry, accounts at least in part for the eagerness of adolescents to take up the habit. Thus, there are always new smokers to take the places of those who move into the cancer wards, or die.

Herein we discover another powerful reason for believing that it's a sin to smoke. Smokers give an example to their children and others; this example, if imitated, can lead to the same addiction or worse, causing the same physical damage or worse. For a biblical perspective on this aspect of the smoking question, read 1 Corinthians 8, substituting the word "smoking" for "food" or "meats offered to idols." Paul warns us, "Be careful, however, that the exercise of your freedom does not become a stumbling block to the weak. . . . When you sin against your brothers in this way . . . you sin against Christ. Therefore, if what I [smoke] causes my brother to fall into sin, I will never [smoke] again, so that I will not cause him to fall" (1 Corinthians 8:9, 12-13, NIV).

"The cigarette century is clearly at an end," says William Bennett.[6] I wish I were as certain as he. This much is certain for you personally: no matter how long you have smoked, the cigarette habit *can* be ended, if, with God's help, you are willing to endure the usual withdrawal symptoms. Why not start today? You owe it to your body!

[6]Bennett, "The Cigarette Century."

8

Education: Whose Responsibility?

The year was 1977, and I was looking into the situational climate of our schools and education. Schools all over the country had opened on time, and there were fewer disturbances than in recent years. For one thing, striking teachers had organized no picket lines—quite a change from the preceding year's 152 teacher walkouts.[1] Except for relatively minor resistance in Chicago's Bogan-Marquette Park area, busing seemed to have been accepted in cities where courts had ordered it.

Resistance in Chicago has been ugly, but by comparison with the resistance we have seen in Louisville or Boston's South Park district, it has been mild. We have hoped that it will not last long.

Time observes that busing is no longer "education's most controversial issue." Where it has been court-ordered, cities have eventually accepted it, "either from sheer fatigue," *Time* says, because of "distraction over declining educational standards, or because in some places busing has worked better than expected."[2]

[1]"Teacher Strikes: At Lowest," *U. S. News & World Report*, 19 September 1977, p. 84.

[2]"Back to Busing—Again," *Time*, 12 September 1977, p. 71.

Most citizens will be relieved, including those who strongly suspect that busing has been wrongly imposed upon them by judges and others whose kids attend fancy schools in the suburbs. Resistance harms the children. Little black children are often terrified, when they are surrounded by gesticulating whites. One can only admire their courage, as they walk the gauntlet to the school doors. What do they think about? And what do the white children think about at such times? Everybody knows the answer: they are learning to fear and hate.

In a column published in *The Chicago Defender*, writer Louis Fitzgerald notes that "kids are not born with malice and prejudice against anyone. It is taught." Fitzgerald contrasts the prejudice manifested at the doors of primary schools with the attitudes of men like Gayle Sayers and Brian Piccolo. They were the best of friends, but why should this be considered unusual? Where minds have not been warped by racial prejudice, it is normal. So, "let the kids alone," insists Fitzgerald.[3]

No one who is familiar with the Bible can miss the unintended allusion to similar words of our Lord. Jesus said, "Let the children alone, and do not hinder them from coming to Me; for the kingdom of heaven belongs to such as these" (Matthew 19:14). Who can tell how great an obstacle to faith we put in a child's way by teaching him contempt, or even hatred, for another race of men? We do our children a disservice by imparting to them such crippling attitudes. The damage is done at home, but it manifests itself on the playing field and in the classrooms.

By teaching children prejudice, parents cause them to

---

[3]Louis Fitzgerald, in Joe Black, "By the Way," in *The Chicago Defender*, 12 September 1977, p. 17.

stumble. Our Lord's warning applies here: "Whoever causes one of these little ones who believe in Me to stumble," Jesus says, "it is better for him that a heavy millstone be hung around his neck, and that he be drowned in the depth of the sea" (Matthew 18:6).

Developing prejudices in children isn't the only damage done at home. According to recent studies, student discipline is *the* major problem in many of the nation's schools. *Time* reports that, in Louisville, "a staggering 14,611 suspensions [were ordered] last year (1976), more than half of them from among the 23 percent black portion of enrollment."[4] Proportionately, twice as many black students as whites misbehave to the point of suspension.

What this means, among other things, is that parents, especially black parents, have their work cut out for them. With figures like this before us, it does no good to protest white resistance to busing, or the white flight to the suburbs. The Reverend Mr. Jesse Jackson knows this, and he is campaigning hard in black schools for more substantial values than hair and clothing styles. Self-discipline, says Joe Black, Vice President of the Greyhound Corporation, "will make [blacks] truly competitive in the labor market."[5]

As Christians see it, parents ought to discipline their children, chiefly because God commands it. Says Paul, "Fathers, do not provoke your children to anger; but bring them up in the discipline and instruction of the Lord" (Ephesians 6:4; cf. Hebrews 12:5-8). Discipline means training, with a view to bringing the child under control. Responsible parents do not shrink from punishing their

[4]*Time*, p. 17.
[5]Black, p. 5.

children when necessary. It may not be pleasant, but the benefits to the child are enormous. Among other things, he learns to respond to authority. Children who do not learn this vital lesson will find it extremely difficult to acknowledge the authority of God, and His right to call them to account for the things they do (2 Thessalonians 1:8). The gospel is essentially a call to obedience. But how shall they obey God, who have never learned to obey?

How shall they obey their teachers? Ask any teacher, and he or she will say that discipline is the top problem in the classroom. *Newsweek* quotes California's superintendent of public education, Wilson Riles, as saying that many children now crowding into big city schools are the most difficult in the history of the public school system. Why so? Because their parents do not discipline them at home. Dr. Riles explains, "What we have are parents beset with all kinds of difficulties, [who are] not able or don't know how to take care of their youngsters." The kids are not encouraged to take their studies seriously, and they bring to the classroom "the unruly, irreverent manners of the street."[6]

This is only part of the story. The schools also come in for sharp criticism. Dr. Kenneth Clark, a child psychologist, who has been a member of the New York State Board of Regents for more than ten years, blames the system, especially its incompetent teachers who, protected by their union, can't and don't teach the basics—such as reading and writing.[7] Clark contends that the teachers pass their students—in some cases functional illiterates—up and out of the system.

---

[6]Jean Seligmann, "City Schools in Crisis," *Newsweek*, 12 September 1977, p. 64.

[7]Ibid.

Other critics fault the system for its experiments that don't work, its notion that all that is needed to solve the problems is more money, its permissiveness whereby students take fancy electives instead of tough, traditional courses, and above all its failure to instill values in the students.

This last criticism may not be entirely fair. It raises a vital question: whose job is it to instill values in the nation's children? The biblical answer is plain: that responsibility belongs to parents, and to a lesser extent, to the church. In ancient Israel, parents were commanded to teach their children the Word of God. "You shall teach them [God's statutes] diligently to your sons and shall talk of them when you sit in your house and when you walk by the way and when you lie down and when you rise up" (Deuteronomy 6:7). Moses taught the people of Israel, and they taught their children.

The pattern set by the Old Testament prevailed in the early church. Timothy learned God's Word from his mother and from his grandmother. They taught him moral values. He knew the difference between right and wrong, which is more than one can say for many young people growing up today in America, who have few if any moral values because they did not learn moral values in their homes, where such things should be taught (2 Timothy 3:14-15; cf. 1:5).

In many cases, parents don't teach moral values, because they themselves never learned them. Some of these adults recognize moral issues, but they refuse to take a stand, lest they be making "moral judgments," which they regard with distaste, as if making moral judgments were evidence of a closed mind or something worse.

When adults just like them are entrusted with the education of children whose parents don't teach them the difference between right and wrong, the situation becomes desperate. The children remain unruly and virtually unteachable. In a statement published by the Federal Communications Commission, Commissioner Margita E. White, citing *Black's Law Dictionary*, observes that education in its "broadest and best sense" includes "not merely the instruction received in school or college, but the whole course of training, moral, intellectual, and physical." Commissioner White quotes from the case of the Commissioners of the District of Columbia versus a certain construction company, in which it is stated that education "is not confined to the improvement and cultivation of the mind, but may consist of the cultivation of one's religious and moral sentiments."[8] Thus, children who do not learn moral values either at home or at school may be said to be uneducated, even if they are competent to function in a secular, technological society.

Officials and teachers are becoming increasingly aware of this defect in the system. Says historian Diane Ravitch of Columbia University, "the public school in America today has tried to fill so many desperate needs that it is in danger of becoming a neutral institution—representing nothing, serving no particular interest well, and having no sense of direction. It's lost some of its moral center. . . ."[9] Ravitch thinks that children should be able to learn in school what's right and what's wrong, and the best values of our civilization.

Others agree, but they're not so sure that schools can do

[8]*News* (Washington, D.C.: The Federal Communications Commission, 16 June 1977), Report No. 15174, footnote 2, p. 3.

[9]"How to Get Quality Back into Schools," *U. S. News & World Report*, 12 September 1977, p. 32.

the job alone. Joseph Featherstone, lecturer at Harvard's Graduate School of Education, maintains:

> In one form or another, schools will have to figure out ways of getting parents and others involved in education—not as lynch mobs demanding "back to basics" or budget cuts, but as helpers in finding answers to the very real question: can schools become more qualitative and more selective in priorities, and discard the idea that quantity must always come first?[10]

Two ideas emerge here as essentials: cooperation of parents and a determination of what is quality education. Ruth B. Love, superintendent of schools in Chicago, Illinois, agrees. Because she is working in the system itself, she calls for cooperation from the students also, as if to imply that we cannot lay all of the blame on delinquent parents. Education, Love states, "must be a mutual effort."[11]

Indeed, children whose parents don't bring them up properly do suffer from serious disadvantages. Nevertheless, children begin early in life to make choices. In the hands of a good teacher, they can be made to understand the nature of the choices they must make, as well as the consequences of the respective choices. Some kids misbehave in school, refusing to do their work, just because they want to misbehave. The notion that there is "no such thing as a bad kid" is pure sentimentalism.

We must distinguish between unmanageable kids and those who, for a variety of reasons, are simply poor students. In such cases, teachers must make extra efforts

[10]Ibid., pp. 32-33.
[11]Ibid., p. 34.

to prepare them for the years after leaving school. It's a tall order, and no doubt we expect too much from teachers. They can teach courses, communicating knowledge to the extent that the student is able and willing to take it in. But they can scarcely be held responsible for a student's character—which, in the long run, has a lot more to say about the student's adult life than a few courses taken in school. Character begins forming before the student goes to kindergarten, and the direction it takes is determined by influences in the home rather than by experiences in school.

So we return to the place where we began—the influence of the home. At home, a child learns prejudice or respect for others. At home, a child learns to respond to authority, or he fails to learn this great lesson. The alternative is lawlessness and its inevitable attendant miseries. When Paul said that the law demanding obedience to one's parents was the first commandment with a promise of blessing, he implied the contrary: refusal to honor one's parents brings retribution, and that in a variety of forms (Ephesians 6:1-3), including, no doubt, academic failure.

Thus, Carolyn Warner, superintendent of public instruction of the state of Arizona, speaks accurately when she says, "parents simply *must* once again come back into the educational process."[12] As Christians and Bible students, we add that the learning process begins at home with moral instruction. Failing in this, parents will find that participation in P.T.A. meetings or any other part of the educational process will be virtually useless.

[12]Ibid.

9

Moral Values and Public Schools

Not too long ago, my wife told me that she had just seen a pornographic movie. It was late, and I was sleepy, so I wasn't sure I had heard her correctly. When I asked her to pass it by me a second time, she explained. In response to repeated invitations from friends, she attended a meeting of the West Suburban Pro-Life Group near Chicago, at which the movie was shown. The flyer announcing the meeting said that viewing the movie was "a must" for every parent of a teen or preteen.

We have no teens or preteens, but I am glad that Naomi attended the meeting, despite the lingering mental distress that accompanies exposure to a pornographic film. The movie is shown in public schools; as taxpayers—the lion's share of whose property taxes goes to support the schools —we are entitled to know what is going on. As Christians, we are morally obliged to know what is being presented to the children in our public school system.

The movie is titled "About Sex," and sex is its subject. Here is what the *National Right to Life News* has to say about it: "You've heard that the movie, 'About Sex' . . . is a real shocker. Well, it is. Unbelievably so. But you'll have to see it yourselves. No way, no way can the full description be published in a family newspaper." The article notes that the movie portrays "every kind of sexual relationship, normal or perverted, complete with gutter talk, back alley language, nudity, crudity, the whole bit," and observes that, if it were shown in a commercial theater, "it would be X-rated [and] the kids wouldn't be allowed to see it." However, it is shown to kids in the public school system.

How is this possible? The answer: it is sponsored by "that socially impeccable institution, Planned Parenthood." One of Planned Parenthood's causes is abortion-on-demand, which probably accounts for the scene in the film in which a woman doctor explains that "doctors like myself, properly trained, can do abortions safely and legally, without any complications for very little cost." The scene shifts to a pretty young girl who tells about how she was aborted painlessly, and thereby rid of an "unplanned" fetus. The girl claimed that she rather liked the idea of motherhood, but not yet; her children would be *planned*.

The movie endeavors to teach girls how to "plan," which really means how to prevent conception while being sexually active. It does not seem to occur to the producers of the movie that chastity—abstinence before marriage—is commendable, or even an option. A basic assumption is that sexual activity is both right and healthy. As Frances Frech observes, "Throughout the movie there is no mention of sex as the foundation of family life. Always the emphasis is on pleasurable stimuli, on 'feeling good.' "[1] The contrast between this view of sex and the biblical treatment of the subject is striking and familiar.

Nobody would fret much about it, if it were just a "porno" movie being shown in sleazy theaters. Paul was

[1]Frances Frech, "Planned Parenthood 'About Sex' Film Called an X-Rated Shocker," *National Right to Life News*, January 1976, p. 6.

realistic enough to say that, in his times, the only way to avoid contact with immoral people would be to leave the world altogether (1 Corinthians 5:10).

Realism in *these* times admits that pornography cannot be stamped out. We are all potentially lewd; lust is part of fallen human nature, and there will be those who pander to it. But it should be possible to *control* pornography—at least to the extent that our children can be protected in the formative years of their lives. There may be no way to protect them completely—no foolproof way to keep the flesh-peddlers at a distance. But it should be possible to protect them from exposure to sexually explicit films in the public schools. If not, what shall we say about the schools?

Planned Parenthood seems to get Frech's harshest criticism: "Gutter talk, perversion, VD, destruction of family values, distortion of facts and ideas, abortion—put them all together and they add up to Planned Parenthood. . . ." But listen to Frech's conclusion: "The milk from the Sacred Cow (i.e., Planned Parenthood) is poisonous, bitter, as unhealthy and addictive as any legal drug. Yet we are allowing our children to be fed on a formula made from it." That statement indicts us as parents and grandparents. We *allow* professional educators—whether in schools or auxiliary institutions such as Planned Parenthood—to divest our children in some cases of the moral values taught them at home and in church, and to substitute values they deem appropriate instead.

This is, in fact, a double indictment. The schools are accused of meddling where they have no right to meddle, and parents are accused of passively accepting the interference with their right to instill moral values in their children. If the charges are true, some schools are dangerous places for children—at least morally. Furthermore, parents who send their children to schools that undermine their spiritual health may be delinquent parents.

Undoubtedly, we are simplifying the question. The schools are a kind of microcosm of society. Spiritually bankrupt teachers (and we have thousands of them) are probably more typical of modern American society than the churchgoer one occasionally finds in the classroom. Many teachers (perhaps even *most* teachers) come from homes in which little attention was given to the inculcation of moral values. Society itself does not know where it gets its values, except to point vaguely to America's "Judeo-Christian heritage." Ask people what that means; in many cases they can't tell you; they don't know *why* they believe what they think they believe. Thus, they have no complaint about moral education in the schools.

This may be an oversimplification. Several years ago, a national news magazine reported that parents and educators were battling over what should be taught in schools. The report said that parents were "on the march in one community after another with increasing successes."[2] Yet the article confirmed the impression that society in general has been aroused only by the schools' failure to teach the basics—reading, writing, and arithmetic. True, there has been plenty of agitation to remove certain textbooks from the curricula, but evidence reveals that parents behind this push are—for the most part Christians who are concerned about their children's moral welfare. Readers may recall the fight over textbooks in West Virginia's Kanawha County. There the prime mover was a Christian woman, Mrs. Alice Moore. The fact that Christians were also behind the agitation in Florida's Dade County is clear

[2]"Parents vs. Educators: Battle over What's Taught in Schools," *U. S. News & World Report*, 19 July 1976, pp. 38-39.

from an editorial broadcast by Miami's WPLG radio station, which took issue with statements made by certain "fundamentalists."[3.]

Should Christians protest what they regard as the failure of the public schools? Our right to do so is questioned only by those educators who think that they, the professionals, are not subject to scrutiny by lay people. Should we *protest* such people, as Mrs. Alice Moore in West Virginia and the West Suburban Pro-Life Group in the Chicago area claim that we should? Accordingly, they organize meetings to inform any parents who are concerned about the moral training of their children. And they take action.

Several good reasons defend this approach. First, the schools belong to the people, not to the teachers and managers who are paid to run them. Second, parents are responsible for the moral training of their children. Third, losing the schools by default to those whose moral values are radically different from those of the rest of us doesn't make sense. Inaction in the face of evil is as much a sin as wrongdoing (James 4:17). Finally, not every parent can take advantage of the only alternative to the public school system—the private schools.

We must note, of course, that private schools are an alternative that increasing numbers of parents are choosing. Reports indicate that "a striking resurgence is under way among the nation's independent schools."[4] Although tuitions are expensive, more and more parents think the advantages are worth the sacrifice. One of the advantages offered in many private schools is the emphasis on tradi-

[3]WPLG, Miami, Florida, Editorial Broadcast, 24 November 1975.

[4]"It's out of the Doldrums for Private Schools," *U. S. News & World Report*, 31 May 1976, p. 51.

tional moral values. Furthermore, since they are not tax-supported, they depend for their survival upon the confidence of the parents—which means, among other things, that the showing of a film titled "About Sex" is unthinkable.

Relatively few parents are able to take advantage of the private school option. They simply can't afford it. Or they may feel that it is wrong to abandon the public schools to those who would turn them into institutions committed to the socialization of students, rather than instruction in the basic disciplines. In such parents' thinking, to quit without a fight would be to do a disservice to the country and, of course, to all of the children who must attend public schools.

Resisting the takeover of the schools, on the other hand, is seen as a Christian duty. How else can Christians function as "the salt of the earth" in society? The quiet testimony of a godly life may go far to convince a believer's neighbors that the gospel is worth listening to. Only as Christians unite in common purpose and make their voices heard can they check the steady erosion of morals in public life and in such national institutions as the schools.

Failure to do so—whether from indifference, selfishness, or craven fear of getting involved—may cost us our saltiness. Jesus said, "If the salt has become tasteless. . . . It is good for nothing anymore, except to be thrown out and trampled under foot by men" (Matthew 5:13). He also said that we are "the light of the world" (Matthew 5:14). Since that is true, "Let your light shine before men in such a way that they may see your good works, and glorify your Father who is in Heaven" (Matthew 5:16).

The point is clear: salt must act, if it is to be effective, and light must shine, if it is to be seen. This is at least part of the scriptural basis for the activity of people such as the West Suburban Pro-Life Group. They feel that it is pointless to pray for help, unless they are willing to put themselves at God's disposal, as His spokesmen.

John the Baptist rebuked a king for adultery (Matthew 14:4; Mark 6:17-18), and Paul lectured on righteousness and self-control before a Roman governor (Acts 24:25). Both men were willing to let God say what needed to be said—in the tradition of Israel's great prophets of the Lord.

In our times, too, we need men and women who are willing to raise their voices on God's behalf and to protest evil in the land. Permissiveness in sexual matters is surely a great sin. Teaching children self-indulgence is an even greater evil, for which the judgment of God must eventually come. Let us, therefore, speak out and let our lights shine in the deepening darkness. And let us, by taking whatever action may be possible and appropriate, act as salt in a society infested by those who would eat its heart out. It is time we as Christians, from every level in society, and every denominational grouping, took action to protect the minds and souls of our children. If not, someday we may be remembered as salt that lost its saltiness—good for nothing but to be thrown out.

10

Evolution vs. Creationism

Biology teachers are worried. They fear that pressure from fundamentalists who object to the way evolution is taught in the public schools will force changes in the content of science courses. In their opinion, the verdict handed down in the so-called "Scopes II" trial in California—which ordered schools to present evolution as theory, not truth—was a case of the camel getting its nose under the tent; before long, more will follow. The prospect dismays them. Hence, we find a spate of articles by scientists who write to instruct us about evolution. I have on my desk a pile of articles, with titles such as "Creationism Isn't Science,"[1] and "The Folks Who Hate Darwin: What to Say to These People."[2] Having read the reactions of evolutionists to "Scopes II" and to the activity of creationists elsewhere, I am moved to reply.

Let me begin with a disclaimer: I am not a scientist. However, I do read a bit. Consequently, I know that fundamentalists and creationists (most creationists are also fundamentalists) are not all as muddleheaded as their opponents would have us believe. I also know that

[1] Niles Eldredge, "Creationism Isn't Science," *The New Republic*, 4 April 1981, pp. 15-20.

[2] Garrett Hardin, "The Folks Who Hate Darwin," *The Dial*, n.d., pp. 44-51.

scientists are not all as bright and all-knowing as the scientific community would like the rest of us to think.

What is a fundamentalist? According to the dictionary, a fundamentalist is a Christian who emphasizes as fundamental "the literal inerrancy of the Scriptures, the second coming of Jesus Christ, the virgin birth, and physical resurrection."[3] If this definition is accurate, you're listening to a "dyed-in-the-wool" fundamentalist. I believe every one of the four doctrines listed above. I personally am not a scientist, but many fundamentalists are. Why should belief in God as revealed in the Bible be thought incompatible with competence in science? The two attributes are not irreconcilable, notwithstanding the press's habitual reference to fundamentalists as if they were all troglodytes.

Scientists would like us to think they are clinically cool, detached observers who analyze their findings with total objectivity. Alas, scientists are often as woolly-minded as the rest of us. Have you seen Anthony Standen's book, *Science is a Sacred Cow*?[4] Niles Eldredge, curator of the Department of Invertebrates at the American Museum of Natural History in New York, admits that scientists are "not all they're cracked up to be." Among themselves, says Dr. Eldredge,

> arguments become heated. Charges of "straw man," "no evidence," and so on are flung about—which shows that scientists, like everyone, get their egos wrapped up in their

[3]*Webster's Seventh New Collegiate Dictionary*, 1969, s.v. "fundamentalist."

[4]Anthony Standen, *Science Is a Sacred Cow* (New York: Dutton, 1974).

work. They believe passionately in their own ideas, even if they are supposed to be calm, cool, dispassionate, and able to evaluate all possibilities evenly.[5]

Eldredge, who is one of the scientists he describes, goes on to say that the argumentation is good for science, since "seldom has anyone single-handedly evinced the open-mindedness necessary to drop a pet idea."[6]

If I were to stop there, I'd distort Dr. Eldredge's meaning. Eldredge wants it understood that nowhere in the squabbling among scientists "has anyone of the participants come close to denying that evolution has occurred." They fight about *how* it happened, not *whether* it happened. Hence, creationists who point to bickering among scientists as evidence that the theory of evolution is in doubt distort the facts, says Dr. Eldredge.[7]

Distortion works both ways; evolutionists frequently misrepresent the views of creationists as well. Here is how *Time*'s researchers present the basic tenets of scientific creationism:

> The earth is roughly 10,000 years old . . . the planets, stars and all living things were literally created in six days by a "Designer"; the different species of plants and animals were created, they did not evolve from any other species; a great flood was the chief force that shaped the face of the earth, in the process drowning the creatures now found as fossils.[8]

This presentation is not entirely misleading; creationists

[5]Eldredge, p. 20.
[6]Ibid.
[7]Ibid., pp. 15, 20.
[8]*Time*, 16 March 1981, p. 81.

do believe that the different species of plants and animals were created. However, by no means do all creationists believe that the earth is only ten thousand years old, or that the planets and stars were created in the six-day period described in Genesis 1.

The Bible opens with the grandly simple statement, "In the beginning God created the heavens and the earth." The second verse says that "the earth was formless and void, and darkness was over the surface of the deep; and the Spirit of God was moving over the surface of the waters" (Genesis 1:1-2). This is really all the Bible says about origins. The rest of the chapter is concerned with God's creative work of fitting the earth for habitation. Between the second and third verses of Genesis 1 is ample room for the millions of years indicated by modern dating methods.

Not all creationists accept the possibility that aeons could have elapsed between the creation of the heavens and the earth, and the creative activity described in verses 3-31 of Genesis 1. The possibility is strongly rejected by spokesmen for the Institute for Creation Research. Prominent among them is Dr. Henry M. Morris, a competent scientist (as are many creationists who disagree with him), who considers the theory just set forth as "impossible scientifically" and "destructive theologically."[9]

The point here is that disputes among evolutionists have their counterpart among creationists. Evolutionists agree that everything evolved from something, but they bicker about the method. They don't agree about how it took place. Creationists, on the other hand, agree that God created the heavens and the earth and stocked the earth

[9]Henry M. Morris, *The Genesis Record* (Grand Rapids: Baker, 1976), p. 46.

with life. But they disagree about how He did it, or how long it took.

Creationists are not anti-science. After all, science is systematized knowledge. Near the end of the nineteenth century, Emil DuBois-Reymond, Professor of Medicine at the University of Berlin, said that "Modern science, paradoxical as it may sound, has to thank Christianity for its origin."[10] DuBois-Reymond was not a Christian; in fact, he strongly rejected supernaturalism. Nevertheless, he acknowledged the debt science owes to the Bible. By de-demonizing the world and freeing it from myths about the gods, the Bible opened the way to scientific investigation. Others have noted that the basic assumptions that made scientific enquiry possible—namely, that there is order in the universe and linkage between the various forms of life—are eminently biblical.

What creationists object to is not science, but scientism, or pseudoscience. In the name of science, evolutionists propagate a view of origins they cannot prove. The facts don't support it. Yet evolutionary theory, including "the descent of man," or "the ascent of man," as J. Bronowski prefers, is set forth as if the pieces were all in place.[11] This is raw scientism, and to creationists, it's unethical.

Dr. Eldredge would be quick to deny the charge. Says he, "Science is ideas, and the ideas are acknowledged to be merely approximations to the truth. Nothing could be further from authoritarianism—dogmatic assertions of what is true."[12] Eldredge's picture of science and scientists

[10]Dubois-Reymond, quoted by Erich Sauer, *The King of the Earth* (London: Paternoster, 1962), p. 86.

[11]J. Bronowski, *The Ascent of Man* (Boston: Little, Brown, 1973).

[12]Ibid., p. 16.

is unrealistically kind. "All science is theory," he explains. Accordingly, "scientists deal with ideas that appear to be the best (the closest to the truth), given what they think they know about the universe at any given moment." The fact that scientists sometimes act as if their notions are the truth should not be unsettling; at such times, says Dr. Eldredge, "they are merely showing their humanity."[13]

Evolutionists do not always give the impression that they believe they are dealing with *ideas;* the impression conveyed to laymen by high school and college textbooks is that evolution is *proved fact.* Jerry Bergman, Ph.D., contends,

> There are dozens of books highly critical of evolutionary theory written either by evolutionists or by individuals who at least do not agree with the creationist position. Rarely does this material find its way into college or high school textbooks or libraries. The result is that few students are aware of the many difficulties in evolutionary theory.[14]

Dr. Bergman believes that "a good education requires that science students at least become *aware* of the basic theories opposing modern evolution theory."

Where will science students learn about problems in evolutionary theory? Not from their teachers. Many—probably most of them at the high school and university undergraduate levels—don't know the problems exist. Dr. Eldredge admits as much. He complains that creationists are "fond of 'debating' scientists by bombarding the typically ill-prepared biologist or geologist with a plethora

---

[13]Ibid.

[14]Jerry Bergman, Ph.D., "Does Academic Freedom Apply to Both Secular Humanists and Christians?" *Impact* (Institute for Creation Research), February 1980, p. 2.

of allegations." If evolutionists get trounced in the debates, says Eldredge, the explanation is that "no scientist is equally at home in all realms of physics, chemistry, and geology, in this day of advanced specialization."[15]

If evolutionists are so sure their theories are truth, they'd better study hard before taking on creationists who know the field and who come prepared to ask hard questions and to pick flaws in the theory.

Creationists don't really want *equal* time in the nation's public schools. Creationists don't dispute true science's findings. I have on my desk a biology textbook prepared by the Creation Research Society.[16] Most of the material in it is standard science. What creationists object to is science's total rejection of supernaturalism, which leads to its unproved view of origins. Science begins with the assumption that God does not exist, or that, if He exists, He had nothing to do with origins. Accordingly, everything that science can learn is made to support the original assumption.

Dr. Eldredge points to a "pattern of similarity interlocking the spectrum of millions of species, from bacteria to timber wolves." For scientists, this proves evolution. For creationists, however, it proves only that all forms of life came from the same Designer. Add to the pattern of similarity the immense complexity of so-called "higher forms" of life, and you will have additional evidence of a Designer/Creator.

Can creationists *prove* that God created the world? No. They can no more prove that the world was created than evolutionists can prove that life evolved. As the Bible

---

[15]Eldredge, p. 17.

[16]Harold Slusher, ed., *Biology: A Search for Order in Complexity* (Grand Rapids: Zondervan, 1970).

itself says, "By faith we understand that the worlds were prepared by the word of God, so that what is seen was not made out of things which are visible" (Hebrews 11:3). Ultimately, whether competent scientists or laymen, we hold to creationism because the Bible teaches it, and we believe it. We have another reason as well: fatal flaws in the evolutionary model.

Creationists aren't asking for equal time to prove that God created the world. All they ask is a chance to present a model that makes as much sense as any alternative, and a little candor among evolutionists. Is this too much to ask?

11

Protest or Unplug the TV—Which?

A few years ago I read that a major network had scheduled the showing of a film featuring incest between a mother and son. I was not surprised. Having discovered that the exploitation of sex is financially profitable, the television industry has been determined to exploit it. The rub is, even the most explicit sex scenes eventually bore an initially rapt audience. The most voracious appetite for pornographic visuals gets jaded. But it can be stimulated, at least temporarily. Count on it; sooner or later virtually everything that can be done sexually will be shown on TV. The viewing audience will demand it.

Meanwhile, the industry is nourishing the public appetite for sordid things. It does this in two ways: first, by producing and showing even more daring films; second, by defending trash with the cant so characteristic of their class. For example, since incest takes place, since it is part of "the human condition," television seems "morally obliged" to "explore" it. Furthermore, we are told, a very explicit scene is not really about sex; it deals with a young man's emotions.[1]

[1]Harry F. Waters, "Does Incest Belong on TV?" *Newsweek*, 8 October 1979, pp. 101-2.

That kind of talk deceives only those who do not know God. Paul would probably include it in his list of "doctrines of demons" (1 Timothy 4:1). Much of what the industry (i.e., its script writers, producers, directors, et al.) defends as "art," Paul would invariably term "filthiness and silly talk, or coarse jesting" (Ephesians 5:4). He would warn us as Christians not to listen to it, and certainly not to watch it dramatized, lest our minds be corrupted by it (2 Corinthians 11:3). That would probably be Paul's first objection to exposure to such things; they defile the mind. They insinuate images that are not easily effaced by the mind.

Paul's second objection to films that pander to eroticism in human nature is that they virtually compel God to come in judgment. Paul warns us not to be gulled into thinking that the immorality of the secular world is harmless: "Let no one deceive you with empty words, for because of these things the wrath of God comes upon the sons of disobedience" (Ephesians 5:6). What does Paul mean—that God judges disobedient people when they die? Yes, but more than that. Scripture teaches what history confirms—that the wrath of God takes various forms and is experienced even in life. God has so made the moral universe that persistence in sin brings its appropriate penalty. That is true of nations as well as individuals. Under the wrath of God, nations die.

That fact, stated in the Bible and confirmed in experience, more than justifies the concern felt by a Methodist minister residing in Mississippi, and the so-called "TV watchdog group" he directs. Learning that the TV network was going to show the incest film, the group's members sent more than 10,000 letters of protest to the network headquarters. They also sent letters to the network's top advertisers, expressing concern that such companies would finance a trashy film.

The conflict raises certain questions of interest. First, is incest an appropriate theme for family viewing? I have already given you my opinion. A network executive disagrees. Says he, "We feel that TV can deal with any sensitive subject if it does so tastefully." Yet, under pressure, the producers cut from the film a sequence showing the mother "passionately kissing her son, and then starting to undress, as both move into the bedroom."[2] You may decide for yourself whether that is a tasteful presentation of a sensitive subject. In my judgment, words such as "sensitive," "tastefully," and "mature" are verbal smokescreens calculated to deceive the simpleminded.

The networks complain that people like the Methodist minister are narrow-minded would-be censors. If they have their way, the networks contend, topics such as incest will never be shown. More verbal smokescreens! The truth is, the group in question—which I take to be representative of most Christians and, no doubt, many non-Christians in the United States—does not object to documentary-style presentation of topics such as incest. A genuine documentary could not help but reveal some of the misery of people trapped in sin. TV dramas, on the other hand, usually (if not always) present the material sympathetically. Thus, they are as deceitful as cigarette advertising, which *never* takes you to the cancer ward— the last stop of many chronic smokers.

Here is another question (as formulated by *Newsweek*'s reporter): "Is a pressure group . . . a legitimate vehicle

[2]Ibid., p. 101.

for viewer protest or a threat to the viewing rights of others?" Television producers claim that pressure on advertisers deprives them (i.e., the producers) of their constitutional freedom to make the kind of movies they want to make. They also complain that it prevents non-protesting viewers from seeing those films. Thus, the producers say, a few protesters are attempting to impose their view of morality on the rest of the country.

At first glance, these appear to be valid objections to the unsuccessful campaign to keep that incest film off the air. Certainly Christians do not wish to impose their view of morality on their unwilling neighbors. In a passage dealing with discipline in the church, Paul says that judging the conduct of unbelievers is not the business of the church. "For what have I to do with judging outsiders?" he asks. "Those who are outside, God judges" (1 Corinthians 5:12-13).

However, the Methodist minister and his group, though Christians, do not protest *as Christians;* they protest *as American citizens*. Says the minister, "I believe we represent millions of Americans who are disgusted with TV. The public is supposed to control the airwaves. Instead, they're controlled by three networks and about three hundred Hollywood writers and producers . . ."[3]

I don't know whether he has his facts straight—whether he and his friends do indeed represent "millions of Americans," or only a few thousand. I suspect that his sympathizers do number in the millions, as he says. In any case, the action taken by the group is perfectly legal and, by comparison with a strike by workers in any industry in the country, quite harmless. It is in no sense disruptive. That incest film was aired, and in all likelihood the

[3]Ibid., p. 102.

96

network will show it again after a suitable lapse of time. For every advertiser who dropped the show, a replacement was found.

The complaint by television people that pressure on advertisers infringes on their right to make the kind of movies they want to rings hollow. It is as if General Motors were to protest that Ralph Nader's campaign to force GM to redesign the Corvair or remove it from production violated their right to make an unsafe car. This kind of complaint raises questions about the very nature of freedom, and certainly about its extent. If nobody is free to shout "Fire!" in a crowded theater, and if nobody is free to manufacture an unsafe car, why should anybody be free to make morally pernicious movies? Hardly anyone who thinks seriously about it can deny that the framers of the United States Constitution and the Bill of Rights did not foresee the kinds of freedom claimed by diverse groups in our times. If they had anticipated real abuse of freedom, they might have incorporated into their work a few lines from the first epistle of Peter. Says Peter, "Act as free men, and do not use your freedom as a covering for evil, but use it as bondslaves of God. Honor all men; love the brotherhood, fear God, honor the king" (1 Peter 2:16-17).

The television industry probably worries more about 250 letters to advertisers than 10,000 letters to the network headquarters. Why? Because their money comes from advertisers who sponsor the shows. Advertisers pay plenty for the privilege of catching your eye and ear for a few seconds. They are willing to risk boring you or sending you to the kitchen for potato chips. But they are not willing to anger you, lest you refuse to buy their products. Hence, they are concerned when picketed, or merely threatened by a sizable group.

Is this kind of pressure legitimate? At least two considerations commend the method: first, pressure on advertisers is probably the only effective way to catch the attention of television executives. Second, three or four networks hold complete control of the airwaves. If you don't like what they produce, you have no alternative—except radio or, better yet, a good book. If you want to watch television, you are stuck with the same fare no matter which channel you tune in, unless, of course, you live in the viewing area of a Christian station. The three major networks strive mightily to outdo each other in producing programs that will appeal to the widest audience, especially at prime time.

This sounds very nice and democratic. The rub is, those three hundred Hollywood writers and producers who churn out the material you see on TV seem to make at least two assumptions that many find questionable: first, that the mental age of their viewers, including adults, is about ten. This probably explains the inane sit-coms in which creatures in various stages of arrested mental development mill about or babble what is supposed to be dialogue. Have you ever personally known anybody like the one-dimensional characters that people your television screen?

The second assumption made by Hollywood writers and producers is that *their* morality, or *their* perception of what is appropriate and good, either meets with the approval of the American people or is good for them. They complain loudly and bitterly about a Methodist minister who can do no more than persuade a few likeminded people to write letters or boycott a powerful industry. They protest indignantly that he is trying to impose his code of morals on them, whereas the truth is just the opposite: the writers and producers, using the

98

all-pervasive and persuasive medium of television, have for years been imposing their warped set of values on the American people. If, as perceptive commentators regularly point out, it is true that traditional values are losing their grip on the American people, whose fault is it? At least part of the blame—a sizable part—rests on the shoulders of the men who determine the kind of programs the people may watch. They have used the medium entrusted to them to corrupt their viewers.

That is one side of the question. The other side concerns the very real sin of the American people in permitting the steady erosion of traditional (i.e., biblical) values. Nobody forces anybody to watch unsavory programs. If we expose ourselves day after day to material completely lacking in moral content, or material that is implicitly or explicitly immoral, whose fault is it if our hold on God and, of course, on spiritual values, slackens? (See Hosea 4:6-9.) And who is to be surprised?

I don't know whether write-ins (letters to network executives and to advertisers), pickets, or boycotts will work. However, I know what *will* work: unplug the set, or turn it off when something objectionable is being aired. Turning it off may not stop the producers from producing mindless or salacious material, but it most certainly will keep you from exposure to it. And that—separation from what is evil—is precisely the path God intends for you (and me) to follow.

12

Should Treatment Be Terminated?

Several years ago Karen Ann Quinlan "passed out" at a party. She never recovered consciousness, but today she is still alive, existing in what doctors term a "chronic vegetative state." Doctors doubt that she will ever wake up. Even if she does, her chances of living a normal life are "as close to zero as you can come without being zero."[1]

Then why go on living? The answer is, Karen Ann Quinlan's continued existence is not an issue over which she or anybody else has control. True, she could be starved to death. If intravenous feeding devices were removed, the girl would quickly die. But who is going to request or authorize that move? Nobody, and rightly so, since it would be regarded as homicide by deliberate neglect. It would be an act of euthanasia, or "mercy killing."

In 1976 the situation was different. A respirator was keeping Karen Ann alive. The girl's parents watched her vegetate for a year, and doctors offered no hope that she would ever recover. The Quinlans went to court for authorization to disconnect the respirator. What they wanted was not termination of customary treatment of

[1]Dr. Julius Korein, "Karen Ann Quinlan—Five Years Later," quoted in *Chicago Tribune*, 29 March 1981.

comatose patients; they wanted an end to heroic measures that kept their daughter breathing yet contributed nothing to her recovery. The machine blocked her passage into eternity. The Quinlans believed that to disconnect it would not be an act of euthanasia, or deliberate killing; it would be "the abandonment of an attempt to restore life."[2]

The New Jersey Supreme Court weighed the issues and handed down a ruling. The court permitted the removal of Karen Ann from the respirator. It was not expected that she would survive the move. Thus, in requesting the ruling her parents expressed their conviction that existence under the circumstances was not in Karen Ann's best interests; death was preferable. In granting the request, the court concurred, and acknowledged the girl's right to die with a minimum of fuss when there was no longer any hope of regaining consciousness.

But, as Fr. John J. Paris contends, "The physician on the case thwarted the will of the court and the parents and continued Karen Ann on the respirator for six weeks until she could be successfully weaned from it."[3] The result? Years later Karen Ann is still alive, and still comatose.

The case raises more questions than we shall have space to ask, much less consider. However, sooner or later all of us may be forced to consider at least two important questions: first, when, if ever, should treatment of a living patient be terminated, and, second, who decides? The sooner we deal with these questions the better. In a crisis, clear thinking is not easy; one's emotions tend to befuddle

[2]A. V. Campbell, *Moral Dilemmas in Medicine* (Edinburgh and London: Churchill Livingstone, 1972), p. 176.

[3]John J. Paris, "Brother Fox, the Courts and Death with Dignity," *America*, 8 November 1980, p. 283.

the mind. But these questions tax the mind under the best of circumstances. My immediate objective, therefore, is not to provide answers but to encourage you to think about the issues.

I hereby go on record as being unwilling to be kept alive by extraordinary methods beyond a reasonable hope of recovery. Why do I take this position, and why go on record? First, let me state the position briefly yet with sufficient precision to avoid misinterpretation. The position is refusal to be kept alive by extraordinary means when brain death has occurred. Under such circumstances, it would be preferable to let nature take its course, resulting in an end to the spontaneous circulation of the blood and breathing. Nearly everybody holds this position. Yet, increasingly it is becoming necessary to say so, as in a "living will." Otherwise, you may end up "plugged in."

Some listeners may question whether it is possible to continue living after brain activity ceases. The answer is yes, unless *all* brain activity has ceased. Karen Ann Quinlan is still alive because not all of her brain activity has ceased. Though the cerebral cortex, which "enables rational self-consciousness," is evidently destroyed, the lower centers of the brain remain unimpaired. These control certain spontaneous vital functions. Consequently, some comatose patients—including Karen Ann Quinlan—continue living for years, though none has lived longer than seventeen years after lapsing into unconsciousness.[4] Professor G. R. Dunstan insists that such persons are not "kept alive"; they *live*.[5]

[4]Korein, p. 8.

[5]Gordon R. Dunstan, *The Artifice of Ethics* (London: Allenson, 1974), p. 89, quoted by Norman Anderson, *Issues of Life and Death* (Downers Grove, Ill.: Inter-Varsity, 1977), p. 101.

As long as they live, they are entitled to elementary nursing care, including regular feeding, bathing, and turning in bed. This is what Karen Ann Quinlan receives, in addition to daily visits from her parents. Joseph Quinlan talks to his daughter, though she never responds or gives any indication that she hears him. He persists, and, he says, "I always tell Karen I'll pray for her. You never know if a comatose person can hear you and if they might wake up."[6]

Why would everybody—or nearly everybody—rather die than live indefinitely on a respirator or other life-support machine? I can find at least two reasons: first, for believers, at least, clinging to life at all costs, under any circumstances, is not the highest value. In his old age, Paul said he was torn between two alternatives: either to go on living in the body, with its potential for fruitful service for God, or to "depart and be with Christ, for that is very much better" (Philippians 1:23). For Paul, death was not the end; it was departure for a better place.

Earlier, an old man named Simeon expressed the same idea. As he cradled the baby Jesus in his arms, he recalled a revelation to his heart that he would not die until he had seen the Messiah. With the baby before him, Simeon prayed, "Sovereign Lord, as you have promised, you now dismiss your servant in peace" (Luke 2:29, NIV).

This brings me to my second reason for preferring death to apparently mindless existence on a respirator: its *apparent* meaninglessness. Did you notice that I said "apparent" or "apparently" twice? This was deliberate. A person in a coma appears to be as unthinking as a baby locked in a dreamless sleep. But we don't really *know* that

6Quoted in Korein, p. 8.

this is the case. More to the point, we don't know whether God communicates with a comatose person. "You never know if a comatose person can hear you," Joseph Quinlan says. He may be wiser than some of his daughter's doctors who evidently think she is a vegetable.

In either case, it isn't true that existence on a respirator is utterly devoid of meaning. For Karen Ann Quinlan, the past years may indeed have been meaningless, lost years. Yet for others, notably her parents, the girl's predicament has been and continues to be meaningful. It has caused them much suffering, and the suffering has contributed to their spiritual maturity. Though it cannot be said that God *wanted* Karen Ann Quinlan to lie helpless for many years, it can be said (and proved from Scripture) that He wants something good to happen as a result of her misfortune. To the extent that any person's sufferings contribute to that person's *or to another person's* spiritual maturity, the sufferings are meaningful. Thus, Karen Ann's existence in a "chronic vegetative state," as some of her doctors judge it to be, may be a lot less meaningless than it appears.

Nevertheless, nobody would wish a similar predicament on anybody, especially himself, notwithstanding its potential for meaning. I do not wish to lie unconscious for weeks or months, and I do not wish to burden my family with unnecessary suffering. Life brings much unavoidable suffering; nobody needs an additional load *created* by medical technology. Everybody is grateful for technology's benefits. Modern medicine saves many babies who would otherwise die, and it keeps most of us healthier than our grandparents for longer lives than they enjoyed. But technology also has its drawbacks, especially its potential for keeping bodies breathing long after they should have been allowed to die.

It's time to think about death. We often hear reference to a Christian view of life. There is also a Christian view of death. These respective views complement each other. Nobody can satisfactorily answer questions about terminating life unless he understands the respective Christian views of life and death, and keeps both views in balance. According to these views, having been conceived and born, we have a right to life, and an obligation to handle life reverently. However, as Christians, we reject the notion that one is *entitled* to death with dignity. There is no such thing as the right to die. We die because we *must* die. The Christian view of life as a gift from God precludes the possibility of our having a say in how and when we die. We cannot determine the manner or the timing of death. Nobody has the right to rush death either by suicide or by refusing reasonable treatment.

The crux of the issue of terminating treatment is our definition of terms such as "reasonable treatment," and "extraordinary means." Thoughtful doctors wrestle with this problem. Treatment that would have been deemed *most extraordinary* a few years ago may be quite common now, and, therefore, reasonable. Twenty years ago, kidney transplants were extraordinary; therefore, only youthful patients who were very reluctant to die would subject themselves to the discomforts of a chancy operation. Now, however, kidney transplants are routinely successful. Doctors do not shrink from requesting kidneys from living donors. Thus, in some procedures, at least, the difference between extraordinary and routine treatment is time—time for the extraordinary to become ordinary and routine.

What this means is that patients must rely on their doctors for the knowledge they need in order to distinguish between routine or reasonable treatment and extraordinary means, before they can decide what to do. In coma cases, the patient's wishes are not known. What then? Someone must exercise what is termed "substituted judgment," which takes into account the patient's known values. But sometimes, even alert, rational patients will refuse reasonable treatment. They prefer death to suffering. What then?

Professor Thomas C. Oden insists that *four* parties, not just the patient—must concur unanimously before active treatment may be terminated. These are the patient, the patient's family, the attending physician, and a hospital ethics committee.[7] If the patient is in a coma, the three remaining key parties will exercise substituted judgment. If the patient is rational yet obsessed by a death-wish, his preference is not sufficient. Responsible doctors would not terminate reasonable treatment at the request of a rational patient, even if the patient's family concurred. There must be more compelling reasons than suffering or despair for terminating treatment.

Thomas Oden believes there is "no definable point at which Jewish and Christian consciousness can say that the value of relieving suffering becomes greater than the value of life itself."[8] Professor Oden speaks as a Christian; he sees life as a gift from God. It is neither to be despised nor thrown away. When Jesus began His work, He preached the gospel *and* He healed the sick (1 Peter 3:7; Luke 6:18; Mark 1). He kept people alive who, without his help, would have died prematurely.

[7]Thomas C. Oden, *Should Treatment Be Terminated?* (New York: Harper & Row, 1976), p. 11.

[8]Ibid., p. 74.

However, He was selective; at the pool of Siloam only one man was healed (John 5:1-14). And none of Christ's "patients" was *permanently* healed. Sooner or later, all of them died—including Lazarus, whom He had raised from the dead. Like Simeon, they died when God let death claim them—no sooner and no later. No doubt many of them died the way God wanted them to die; certainly none committed suicide.

Jesus told Peter that when he was younger he did more or less what he wanted to do. "When you are old," the Lord said to him, "you will stretch out your hands, and someone else will gird you, and bring you where you do not wish to go." What did Jesus mean?

John explains: "Now this He said, signifying by what kind of death he [Peter] would glorify God" (John 21:18-19). Ah, that's the way to go: *when* God wills it, and *how,* and *in such a way* as to give glory to God.

Should treatment be terminated? A better question is this: what kind of treatment should be started in the first place? For, once treatment has been started, doctors must have adequate cause for stopping it. Relief of pain and suffering is not adequate cause, according to Christian principles. Only one cause truly justifies discontinuing routine, reasonable treatment. What is it? Death, which sooner or later claims us all.

13

On Capital Punishment

Two items in the newspaper some time ago drew fresh attention to the subject of capital punishment: first, reports of demonstrations in Atlanta against capital punishment, and, second, the trial in San Francisco of "an honest and conscientious young political leader, a dedicated family man and a devout Catholic," who, nonetheless, had been charged with the murders of two men, including San Francisco's mayor.[1] My comments are a response to the demonstrators.

The point of view is biblical. What do the Scriptures teach about capital punishment? First, let me explain that I *try* to approach the Scriptures with that combination of reverence and detachment that is necessary if one is to reach an understanding of the truth. Reverence comes easily; I believe the Bible is the Word of God. Detachment is more elusive. When thinking about hardened criminals or mass murderers, I am conscious of an emotional commitment to the death penalty. Men who leave bombs in hotel lobbies, in this way killing or maiming innocent passersby, should be eliminated. On the other hand, I am also conscious of the irreversibility of the death penalty; it ends forever the lives of all who taste it.

[1]Michael Coakley, "San Francisco Murder Trial Fails to Answer: Why?" *Chicago Tribune*, 13 May 1979.

I have on my desk a recent letter from a pen pal who killed a policeman in a shootout during an attempted bank robbery. He was convicted of murder, but because the crime took place after the United States Supreme Court's ruling that capital punishment is "cruel and unusual," he was sent to prison for life. A few years later he became a Christian. Suppose he had been sentenced to death?

Questions such as this do not have much bearing on the subject; they just remove the subject from the realm of the abstract. Normally, men sentenced to death have plenty of time to review their lives and think about meeting God. If a condemned man does not get saved in the time allotted, why should it be thought that he would eventually repent if given additional time, or, in the cases of those sentenced to life in prison, unlimited time? Bible students generally believe that God gives every man as much time as he needs or wants to repent and believe the gospel. According to this belief, if my pen pal had been sentenced to death, he would have thought seriously about his soul's eternal destiny a whole lot more quickly than he did. Hence, his conversion in prison is not pertinent to the question.

What does the Bible teach? Christians disagree; the question is uncommonly complex, and naturally believers range themselves on both sides of the issue. However, it is easier to make a biblical case *for* capital punishment, than to defend the abolitionist position. Those who believe that the Bible establishes capital punishment usually cite Genesis 9:5-6 in support of their position. Speaking to Noah, God says, "And surely I will require your lifeblood; from every beast I will require it. And from every man, from every man's brother I will require the life of man. Whoever sheds man's blood, by man his blood shall be shed, for in the image of God He made man."

The passage's first purpose affirms the sanctity of human life, as contrasted with animal life. Earlier God had said that it was lawful to kill and eat animals. But human beings may not be killed; their life is sacred. It is so sacred that its violation cannot be expiated except by the life of the murderer. "Whoever sheds man's blood, by man *his blood shall be shed*" (italics added).

It is obvious that the text makes a distinction between murder in cold blood and a legal execution. "*By man* his blood (i.e., the blood of a murderer) shall be shed." The distinction is made possible by the existence of government. Bible students generally agree that the passage before us establishes government as an institution, and charges it with the protection of human life. The protection of human life seems to include two ideas: first, retribution for murder (the murderer must be executed), and, second, determent (the threat of execution prevents potential killers from becoming actual killers).

Taking these ideas in reverse order, one must admit at the outset that opponents of capital punishment deny its deterrent value. They say that data accumulated in studies do not support the claim that capital punishment deters potential murderers. Not many ordinary people believe these studies are valid. Why not? Because, as former Solicitor General of the United States, Robert Bork, says, "The assertion that punishment does not deter runs contrary to the common sense of the community . . ."[2]

Lloyd L. Weinreb, Professor of Law at Harvard, agrees with Bork. Says Weinreb, "The easier it is to get away with . . . murder, the less the deterrent effect on those who are inclined to attempt it. This is still good common

[2]Quoted by George F. Will, "In Cold Blood," *Newsweek*, 29 November 1976, p. 116.

sense. If it were not, we should posthaste liquidate the whole law enforcement establishment as a useless, misguided effort to control human conduct."[3]

The refusal to acknowledge the deterrent effect of the death penalty is astonishing. George F. Will observes that "there is ample evidence that the rates of many specific crimes are related negatively to the likelihood of punishment and its severity." Will cites a statistical study that indicates that each execution "may save as many as eight lives."[4]

From a biblical point of view, determent is a by-product of punishment. It is not the primary objective. It would be immoral—from a biblical perspective—to execute a man who might otherwise escape the death penalty *just* to make others think twice before committing the same crime. The prophet Ezekiel makes this point clearly. Says he, "The person who sins will die. The son will not bear the punishment for the father's iniquity, nor will the father bear the punishment for the son's iniquity; the righteousness of the righteous will be upon himself, and the wickedness of the wicked will be upon himself" (Ezekiel 18:20). Under a just system, each person gets what he deserves.

However, in ancient Israel the execution of criminals was expected to do more than punish the offender; it affirmed the principle of law and order in the community. Moses gave instructions for the execution of certain types of offenders, and explained the effect on the community. Said he, "Then all Israel will hear and be afraid, and will

[3]Lloyd L. Weinreb, ed., *Leading Constitutional Cases on Criminal Law* (Mineola, N.Y.: Free Press, 1976), p. 513.

[4]Will, p. 116.

never again do such a wicked thing among you" (Deuteronomy 13:11; cf. 17:13). Thus, an execution must accomplish two objectives: first, its primary objective, which is punishment of the criminal, and, second, determent.

It is no doubt significant that the right (indeed, many Bible students view it as an obligation) to execute murderers is the only function of government mentioned in the passage cited. The explanation is not hard to find: the authority to execute a human being subsumes all lesser powers. If the state is empowered to execute its worst offenders, it can also lock up or fine lesser offenders. In short, divine permission to exact the death penalty carries with it permission to take whatever steps may be necessary to control society's unruly elements.

Control—which is another word for determent—is certainly the main objective of the law. As Paul says, "Law is not made for a righteous man, but for those who are lawless and rebellious" (1 Timothy 1:9). Law is designed to protect society by restraining its selfish or vicious members. When the law fails to prevent crime, it seeks its secondary objective: retribution, or punishment of the criminal. Control then becomes secondary, a by-product of effective administration of punishment.

In some circles, the concept of punishment is in disfavor, unless it can be demonstrated that it contributes something to the rehabilitation of the criminal. Death, of course, does not rehabilitate the criminal; it terminates him. Accordingly, the death penalty is abhorred as barbaric and unjust.[5] Modern man prefers to think of criminals as "sick," rather than guilty, and, therefore, in need

[5] Abe Fortas, "The Case Against Capital Punishment," *New York Times Magazine*, 23 January 1977, p. 9.

of therapy rather than punishment. In a fine essay in *God in the Dock*, C. S. Lewis talks about the menace inherent in such seemingly sweet, harmless notions.[6]

Capital punishment is not designed to cure sick people; its purpose is punishment. In the Bible, there is no connection between punishment and rehabilitation; the connection is between punishment and justice. Justice calls for the punishment of offenders; if the effects are salutary, so much the better. But the primary purpose of punishment is the satisfaction of justice, not reform. Neither Achan (Joshua 7) nor Ananias and Sapphira (Acts 5:1-11) were given time to change their ways. When they refused to relent, they were condemned to death and executed without delay. Justice demanded it.

This is not the whole story, of course. Cases can be cited in which justice relented. King Manasseh was spared the doom he had earned (2 Chronicles 33:12-13) and King David, who also committed capital crimes, was likewise spared (2 Samuel 11-12). In each case, the explanation seems to be their genuine repentance. By denying mercy to some, and granting it to others, God reveals two truths about Himself: first, His wrath against all unrighteousness. God is against sin, and His justice demands that it be punished. Second, He is willing to forgive.

These two concepts would be irreconcilable apart from the cross. The gospel is the story of God's power to reconcile two antithetical concepts—His justice and His mercy. How did He do it? By sending His Son to be made sin "on our behalf," to be treated as if He were sin itself, and punished accordingly. Christ's death was vicarious;

[6]C. S. Lewis, "Is Punishment Deserved?" *God in the Dock: Essays on Theology and Ethics*, ed. Walter Hooper (Grand Rapids: Eerdmans, 1970), p. 287.

He died for us. His death was a demonstration of God's wrath toward sin, and also His love for us. As Paul says, "God demonstrates His own love toward us, in that while we were yet sinners, Christ died for us" (Romans 5:8). Justice demanded a victim and received it in Christ.

Am I saying that justice is inexorable, that it always demands satisfaction? Yes and no, though the question must be deferred. I am saying (1) that human life is sacred, (2) that those who violate it by murder forfeit their own lives, and (3) that the state is the instrument of God's justice. Consequently, the passage of laws that forbid capital punishment cannot be right; they are, in effect, a denial of the biblical view of man as made in the image of God. Laws that abolish capital punishment equate murder with any of a number of lesser social offenses.

Am I now saying that *all* murderers should be hanged, electrocuted, or shot to death? No. When David confessed his crime, Nathan told him that *the Lord* had taken away his sin. When a woman caught in the capital crime of adultery was taken before Jesus, He did not protest the severity of the law, but He did insist on a just application of it. Where was the man who was with the woman when she was caught in the act? The woman's accusers had let him go. By their act they revealed partiality, and demonstrated their moral unfitness to call for the death penalty. The Lord made this truly important point: only the upright qualify as executioners. "He who is without sin among you, let him be the first to throw a stone at her" (John 8:1-11).

Not many citizens would deny that action against the many cold-blooded murderers walking our streets is long overdue. However, only a moral society is fit to exercise the power of taking a life for a life, for only a moral society is capable of assessing guilt properly, a biblical requirement in capital cases (Numbers 35:30). In my judgment, our own society is nearly incapable of exercising this awesome power in the spirit which is required—as those who are truly appalled by murder and believe that murderers should be handed over to God. Here, the national moral fiber is so weakened that we are outraged only by crimes that inconvenience us personally.

Violence amuses us, if our taste for TV is a true guide. I have on my desk an article published by *The Quill*, titled "Death Brought to You Live," a serious discussion of the prospects for television viewing of an execution in a Texas prison.[7] Crimes that don't touch us or our families merely titillate our interest.

What we need is a mighty and far-reaching outpouring of the Holy Spirit of God. Until such an event, let's keep our capital punishment laws intact. Even so, we need not keep the hangman busy; history reveals that nations that do are not infrequently governed by scoundrels who should themselves be hanged.

[7]Dave McNeely, "Death Brought to You Live," *The Quill*, February 1977.

14

Crime and Prison Reform

I have often said that we as a nation do not take crime seriously. True, we talk about crime more than any other society; I suspect that we publish more studies about crime than all other societies combined. But we don't do much about the problem. Witness the fact that crime in the United States is increasing. Whereas crime is not a serious problem in other industrialized societies (e.g., Japan, Taiwan), in our society it has been a serious problem for decades, and it's getting worse.

I return to the subject, not to repeat everything said earlier, but to discuss prison reform and to suggest action that may be taken by the Christian community. My decision to focus on crime was prompted by three events: first, Chief Justice of the United States Supreme Court Warren E. Burger's speech before the American Bar Association, calling for a crackdown on violent crime; second, the American Civil Liberties Union's criticism of the speech; and, finally, Charles E. Colson's participation in a Moody Bible Institute Founder's Week Conference. Colson probably knows as much as any man in the United States about one aspect of the crime problem, the need for prison reform. He knows—from first-hand experience and from wide reading—that the prison system does not rehabilitate offenders; instead, it turns many of its inmates into more accomplished criminals than when first caught and convicted. Colson also knows that some prisoners can be rehabilitated; in fact, many are being rehabilitated through the presentation of the gospel of Jesus Christ. In his Founder's Week message, Colson told how some men were changed by an encounter with Christ.

I wish that Chief Justice Burger had heard Charles Colson's speech before making his own. It might not have made a difference, but it's pleasant to think otherwise. In any case, Burger called for needed changes in the criminal justice system in the United States. He said, among other things, that trials should take place within weeks after an arrest. We Christians have been saying this for years, mainly because of an Old Testament principle: "Because the sentence against an evil deed is not executed quickly, therefore the hearts of the sons of men among them are given fully to do evil" (Ecclesiastes 8:11). In other words, people commit crimes so readily because crime is not punished quickly enough.

The Chief Justice may have been thinking of the legal difficulties caused by long delays between the arrest of a suspect and his trial in court. Before a case comes to trial, key witnesses may have been lost. In some cases, they die; in others, they are intimidated, or they forget the indignation they felt at the time the crime was committed. Having appeared in court once or twice only to hear that the trial is to be "continued," they lose interest. The result? A criminal who might have been convicted is freed. In all likelihood, he will commit another crime.

The ACLU agreed that suspects should be given speedier trials. However, that organization sharply criticized the justice's proposals to limit bail bond to prisoners deemed non-dangerous. At the present, judges are supposed to consider only the probability that a suspect will show up at a later date. Burger noted that many violent crimes are committed by men free on bail and said that judges should be authorized to consider the "future dangerousness" of defendants before granting bail. Most people consider that a reasonable suggestion. However, a spokesman for the ACLU said he was "shocked" by the proposal because (he said) it would "turn the presupposition of innocence entirely on its head."[1]

This is nonsense. The presupposition of innocence was never intended to be taken absolutely. Technically, a criminal caught in the act is presumed innocent until legally convicted. But legal niceties—which were designed to protect the *truly* innocent, not the *technically* innocent —do not (or should not) blind either the arresting officer or the magistrate to known facts. If a man known to be violent in the past appears in court on a fresh charge of violence, only a fool would grant him easy freedom on bail bond. The welfare of potential victims is as important as his presumed innocence. To release a man known to be dangerous would be irresponsible. The ACLU's objection to Chief Justice Burger's proposal that such men be denied bail bond illustrates a well-known facet of human nature: the tendency to evaluate every idea or suggestion according to its real or imagined effect on one's pet ideas.

Nobody seems to have opposed Burger's call for prison reform. No doubt some do oppose it—certainly the "lock-'em-up-and-throw-away-the-key" crowd, the citizens who are justifiably outraged by the indeterminate sentencing that permits the early parole of unrepentant, unreformed criminals. Everybody has heard about at least one monstrous crime done by a man on parole. But locking all offenders up permanently is not the solution to

[1]Quoted by Lee Strobel, "ACLU Criticizes Burger Proposals," *Chicago Tribune*, 10 February 1981.

the problem. For one thing, it ignores a crucially important fact: not all prisoners are unreformable. In every prison there are lots of habitual criminals (recidivists, in technical jargon), and not many citizens care whether these individuals are comfortable or not. However, there are also first-offenders; and there are also second and, conceivably, third-offenders who are still reformable. They are not yet habitual criminals. Prison reform is very urgently needed for their sake.

In this short chapter, I do not presume to tell you what's wrong with American prisons, or what can be done to change them. About ten years ago, Jessica Mitford wrote about the system in a book titled *Kind & Usual Punishment*. It was a best-selling exposé of prisons in the United States. You may have seen it. Since its publication, many other thoughtful studies have been made available to general readers. If you're interested, check the card catalog in your local library. Most of the available material is realistic enough to keep you from thinking the system can be reformed overnight. Meanwhile, there is much the Christian community can do to alleviate the distress of reformable prisoners and their families.

What can we Christians do? Several years ago *Eternity* published an article by Charles E. Colson, "Who Will Help Penitents in Penitentiaries?"[2] Colson listed four things: first, we can visit men and women in prison; second, we can get our local church involved; third, we can support community treatment centers or halfway houses; and finally, we can educate public officials. Most of us recoil from the suggestion that we visit those in

[2]Charles Colson, "Who Will Help Penitents in Penitentiaries?" *Eternity*, May 1977, p. 12.

prison. We don't know anybody in jail, and we don't know anybody who works in a jail. And if we did get permission to visit the prisoners, we wouldn't know what to say to them.

Colson notes what you can easily confirm with a telephone call; if you call the warden of the local prison, you'll probably learn that a group is already at work. I should have said *groups,* plural, since there are several kinds, both secular and religious. Religious groups predominate, I am told. In nearly every jail and prison in the United States there are men and women who serve as chaplains, either as professionals or volunteers.

The point in calling attention to men and women already at work in prisons is to give encouragement to others to join hands with them. I know professionals and volunteers, and they all say that they are overwhelmed by opportunities for service in their respective jails and prisons. They call for helpers. If you're interested in reaching out to reformable prisoners and their families, contact the people already at work in prisons. If they have been at it for an appreciable time—say several years— they know what they are doing, and they can give you advice that may save you frustration and heartache. They can also tell churches how to get involved.

Colson's fourth point is intriguing: he tells us to educate public officials. What he means is, let legislators and others in office know that we are concerned about the prisons. Says Colson, "Few state legislators, U. S. Congressmen and Senators really care about the prison problem because the public doesn't care."[3] He's right, of course. If it weren't for my friends who try to educate me,

[3]Ibid., p. 34.

and a partly awakened Christian conscience, I doubt that I'd care what happens behind bars. None of my friends or their children is in jail. Hence, it's easy to accept the popular notion that all of the men and women in prison are vicious criminals. Yet the testimony of men like Colson and other Watergate figures, and the testimony of prison chaplains and experienced volunteers is that many prisoners are victims rather than victimizers. Moreover, they are salvageable characters. They respond to the gospel of Jesus Christ, and (in some cases) to simple friendship offered with no strings attached.

Surely taking an interest in these people is a Christian response. When Jesus read the Hebrew Bible in Nazareth, He chose a passage in Isaiah with the following lines:

> The Spirit of the LORD GOD is upon me,
> Because the LORD has anointed me
> To bring good news to the afflicted;
> He has sent me to bind up the brokenhearted,
> To proclaim liberty to captives,
> And freedom to prisoners;
> To proclaim the favorable year of the LORD
> (Isaiah 61:1-2; cf. Luke 4:18-19).

Psalm 146 says that "The LORD sets the prisoners free" (v. 7). It's easy to read into these and similar passages what is not there. Certainly the Lord is not sentimental about prisoners, especially those who are dangerous to society. Yet it's impossible to read the Bible without concluding that God hears the groans of prisoners, and cares.

Colson lists a few of the most common prison abuses. The first is disparity in sentencing. One man may get twenty years for the same crime for which his cellmate got a one-year sentence. This, says Colson, quoting a promi-

122

nent law school professor, "is the single greatest cause of bitterness inside America's prisons." Colson asks how we can teach an offender the absolutes of right and wrong when he sees injustices in the nation's courts.

A second abuse is the parole system, mentioned already. Says Colson, "Often, the prison-wise criminal gets out; the less sophisticated offender stays in. For everyone, the suspense is excruciating."[4] The remedy: an end to indeterminate sentencing. Let a man know exactly how many days he must serve time. The testimony of prisoners is that even a long sentence would be easier to endure than the uncertainty of not knowing when the ordeal would end.

Two positive suggestions: the first is for vocational training for prisoners. Henry Fairlie draws attention to the correlation between unemployment, especially unemployment among youth, and incidents of crime.[5] Most offenders are uneducated and, therefore, unemployable. It's useless to release them as unemployable as they were when they entered the prison system. To do so is to doom many, if not most, to a speedy return to prison.

The second suggestion is a search for alternative forms of punishment. The United States prison system is a colossal failure, if its critics are right. Nobody disputes the wisdom of locking up the 20 percent or more who are in prison for crimes of violence. Let them stay where they are. But for the others—thieves, swindlers, and the like, there must be a better, more effective punishment. Fines, public service, restitution—these alternative forms of

[4]Ibid.

[5]Henry Fairlie, "It Is the Law-Abiding People Who Can Do the Most to Create a Crime-Free Society: To Retreat Before Crime Is to Accept It," *The Denver Post*, 25 January 1981.

punishment are worth a try, and, having a basis in Scripture, they just might work.

Colson offers a constructive conclusion:

> God can do the job of ending the abuses and inhumanity of our prisons, of reducing recidivism and crime rates and saving the lost. He needs only those who are called to be His instruments.[6]

If you're interested, the explanation may be that God is calling you to prison ministry.

[6]Colson, p. 36.

Moody Press, a ministry of the Moody Bible Institute, is designed for education, evangelization, and edification. If we may assist you in knowing more about Christ and the Christian life, please write us without obligation: Moody Press, c/o MLM, Chicago, Illinois 60610.